Encyclopedia of
Antique
American
Clocks

Second Edition

Robert W. & Harriett Swedberg

©2004 Robert W. and Harriett Swedberg

Published by

krause publications

An F+W Publications Company

Our toll-free number to place an order or obtain
a free catalog is (800) 258-0929.

Library of Congress Catalog Number: 2004103299

ISBN: 0-87349-807-0

Designed by Gary Carle

Edited by Dan Brownell

Printed in the United States of America

Table of Contents

Acknowledgments.................................4

Introduction.....................................6

Chapter 1 An Overview of Clock Types.......7

Chapter 2 Clocks Through Time.................15

Chapter 3 Histories of Clock Manufacturers 26

Leading Manufacturers 26

    Ansonia Clock Company 26

    William L. Gilbert Clock Company 27

    E. Ingraham Company 28

    New Haven Clock Company 29

    Seth Thomas Clock Company 31

    Waterbury Clock Company.......................32

    E. N. Welch Manufacturing Company 33

    Welch, Spring & Company.......................34

Smaller Manufacturers 36

    E. Howard Clock Company.......................36

    Ithaca Calendar Clock Company 36

    Joseph Ives 39

    F. Kroeber Clock Company 39

    Lux and Keebler 42

    Eli Terry 42

    Willard Brothers 43

Other Small Manufacturers.....................45

Chapter 4 Old Timers.............................46

    Banjo...47

    Grandfather 61

    OG 67

    Shelf..79

Chapter 5 Wall Clocks 90

    Advertising 91

    Calendar 97

    Gallery 109

    Octagon 111

    Wall Regulator 118

Chapter 6 Classic Clocks.................................146

    Crystal Regulator....................................147

    Porcelain 154

    Statue/Figural...167

    Cabinet 179

Chapter 7 Shelf Clocks.....................................180

    Alarm...181

    Black Mantel 191

    Calendar 202

    Carriage...213

    Gothic 215

    Mantel..228

    Metal and Iron Front 241

    Oak..248

    Parlor...260

Chapter 8 Novelty Clocks 286

    Wall...287

    Shelf..293

Chapter 9 Foreign Clocks.................................320

Chapter 10 Useful Clock Information 346

Glossary...358

Bibliography..367

Acknowledgments

The authors sincerely thank the following collectors and dealers who assisted in obtaining photographs and information for this book. We also thank those clock collectors who allowed us to include some of their photographed clocks but did not wish to be listed.

Annawan Antique Alley
Mary Wheeler
Annawan, Illinois

Antique America
Cheryle Fry
Davenport, Iowa

Antique & Specialty Center
Don and Sharon Hanebuth
Anchorage, Alaska

Shafer & Sons Clock Co.
Antique Mall
Rockford, Illinois

Antique Scene
Rachel and Jack Cattrell
Moline, Illinois

Banowetz Antiques
Maquoketa, Iowa
Operated by
Virl and Kathey Banowetz

Marion and Vera Blevins

Gary Bowker

Richard and Norma Broline

Bill and Dora Brubaker

Butterworth Clock Repair
Mark Butterworth
Muscatine, Iowa

Chuck Cline

James Stanley Feehan
Joy, Illinois

Kerry Goodwin

Bennie L. Hack
Decatur, Illinois

Pastor Troy C. Hedrick

Jack Heilsler

Scott Helmich

Carmon M. and
Peggy M. Howe

The Illinois Antique Center
Dan and Kim Philips
Peoria, Illinois

Mort Jacobs Restorations
Chicago, Illinois

J. & S. Antiques & Mall
Jim and Sandy Boender
Manlius, Illinois

Shirley Kilgard

David and Emily Lewis
Specializing in Kroeber clocks
Western Illinois

The Louisville Antique Mall
Harold L., Chuck, and
Don Sego
Louisville, Kentucky

Michael and Patricia Lowe

Majestic Lion
Des Moines, Iowa

Bill and Sandy Mittelstadt

Oldest Son's Antiques and
Appraisal Service
Nancy, Jerry, and helper Jason
Pocahontas, Illinois

Old Timers Antique Clocks
Dick Masters
Louisville Antique Mall
Louisville, Kentucky

Peerless Antiques & Auctions
Chris Wojtanowski
Rock Island, Illinois

Terry and
Gretchen Poffinbarger

Pritts Antiques
Talvia and Theral
Decatur, Illinois

Dennis and Barbara Roberts

Antique Clocks & Repair
Ken Russell
Lacon, Illinois

Smokehouse Square Antiques
Ken and Lesley Denzin
Amana, Iowa

Barry and Lori Snodgrass

John Tanner
Chino, California

Mariam Thornton

Village Square Antiques
Theresa and Glen Nance
Pocahontas, Illinois

Introduction

Clock Collecting: A Rewarding Experience

Clocks are a joy to collect. One of the most satisfying aspects of the hobby is that enthusiasts can choose any number of ways to collect them. For example, some hobbyists collect clocks made by a particular company, like Ansonia or Seth Thomas, while others collect certain styles, such as Gothic, mantel, statue, or calendar. Most clock collectors, however, are eclectic and accumulate a wide variety. But no matter how collectors choose to develop their hobby, clocks provide a way to learn about history and the development of technology. Clock museums give collectors even more opportunities to increase their knowledge by providing the chance for them to see rare examples in person. For the readers' convenience, a number of clock museums are listed in chapter 10.

A Warm Thanks

Since we especially want to help novices expand their knowledge of clocks, we have presented both common and unusual examples but only those found in private homes, shows, conventions, and shops. Some of the clock collectors whose clocks and prices we listed did not wish to be acknowledged, but thankfully, most were willing to share their expertise. We are particularly grateful to those dealers who opened their homes to us, helped arrange their clocks for photographs, and provided background information about them.

What's New

This edition offers a number of improvements over our previous one, including several hundred new photos. And all the photos in the book are color. Also new is a chapter on foreign clocks, whereas the first edition was devoted exclusively to American clocks. The chapter features over fifty foreign examples, including clocks from Great Britain, Germany, France, Austria, and Sweden. In addition, the book has been reorganized to make it even easier to find the information you need. And finally, you'll find a new section in chapter 10 that provides practical advice for handling and selling your clock.

A Note on Pricing

The prices and photographs in this clock guide were provided by private collectors, dealers, and members of the National Association of Watch and Clock Collectors (NAWCC). Because the authors did not set prices on any of the clocks, and because pricing is somewhat subjective, they and their publisher cannot be responsible for the outcome of any sales. The prices are a general guide, not a guarantee of the results of any particular transaction. After all, price guides reflect averages prices of many sales, whereas individual prices can vary greatly. Prices are affected by a number of factors, including location, season, competition, etc. But the bottom line is that any item is only worth what someone is willing to pay for it at a particular time. That's the basic principle that drives a free-market economy.

The three following examples provide a good illustration of the variations you may encounter. Two Ansonia "Queen Elizabeth" mahogany wall clocks are listed with $100 difference in price—$900 in one place, $800 in another. In another case, one dealer listed a Waterbury "Halifax" clock at $600; another listed his at $400. A third, more dramatic example is that of two Ansonia octagon short-drop simple calendar clocks. One is priced at $1,000, the other at $500.

A Word to the Wise

While most dealers are honest, it's wise to take precautions when searching for clocks. For instance, some clocks, particularly at large auctions, are "marriages." In other words, they contain parts from several other clocks. Dishonest sellers may take months preparing bogus clocks for unsuspecting novice buyers. To avoid being cheated, find a reputable dealer to mentor you and reward that dealer by being a loyal customer.

Chapter 1
An Overview of Clock Types

Sessions walnut jeweler's regulator wall clock, advertising Weiler's Music Store, Quincy, Illinois, time only, 1902, 38 1/2" h. **$700**.

Pictured in this chapter are examples of the various types of clocks that are shown and priced throughout this book.

ADVERTISING CLOCK

Advertising clocks display promotional information on their cases, dials, or tablets. Two early U.S advertising clock companies began manufacturing these wall clocks in the late 1800s. The first was the Sidney Advertiser Company of Sidney, New York; the second was the Baird Company of Plattsburgh, New York. Sidney featured a clock with advertising messages placed on a drum that turned every five minutes. Baird's early clock cases were made of papier-mâché; later, they were made of wood.

ALARM CLOCK

Although the Greeks developed a water-operated alarm clock around 250 B.C, the first mechanical alarm clock was not invented until 1787, when Levi Hutchins of Concord, New Hampshire, made a crude model. Because the alarm could only be set to ring at 4 A.M., however, it was of little practical use. In 1876, nearly a hundred years later, Seth Thomas created and patented a wind-up alarm clock that could be set for any hour.

Left, **Ansonia** flower girl alarm clock, 7" h. **$375**.
Right, **Ansonia** cupid alarm clock, 6 1/2" h. **$400**.

BANJO CLOCK

Simon Willard patented his wall clock in 1802. While he called it his "Improved Timepiece," it became known as the banjo clock because of its shape. It featured a pendulum that could be screwed down so the clock could be easily moved without damaging its suspension. Unlike many clocks of that day, the banjo clock is an original design rather than a version of a European clock. Although its popularity diminished after 1860, it has frequently been copied ever since.

BEEHIVE (GOTHIC) CLOCK

Beehive clocks are so named because they resemble the gently curving cone shape of a beehive. They are also known as Gothic clocks because they incorporate the shape of a Gothic arch. These clocks were widely produced by most U.S. clock manufacturers from the 1840s until the early 1900s.

Sessions mahogany finished banjo wall clock w/Sessions on dial, eight-day time & strike, 6" dial, 10 1/2 x 35" h. **$275**.

CABINET CLOCK

The term "cabinet clock" is a rather broad one, referring to a 12- to 24-inch tall, highly polished, shelf clock whose case has been built by a skilled cabinetmaker. Cabinet clocks have hidden pendulums, typically feature oak, ash, walnut, ebony, or mahogany cases, and are eight-day time-and-strike models.

E. N. Welch rosewood beehive (Gothic) shelf clock, all original, ca. 1860 to 1870, 10 1/2 x 19" h. **$350**.

Ansonia "Cabinet C" oak shelf clock, brass dial, ormolu decorations, turned oak columns & brass feet, eight-day time & strike, 11 1/2 x 19" h. **$1,100**.

CALENDAR CLOCK

In about 1853, John Hawes of Ithaca, New York, made the first simple calendar clock in the U.S. Several years later, the first perpetual calendar clocks were produced. Perpetual models are superior to simple ones because they automatically adjust for leap years and differing numbers of days in the months. Most calendar clocks have two dials, one for time and the other for the date.

CARRIAGE CLOCK

Carriage clocks were designed to hang inside coaches and were often covered with leather cases to protect them. They typically feature a rectangular brass case with glass front and sides, a porcelain dial, and a bail-type handle on top. Many also have a smaller subsidiary alarm dial below the main dial.

Seth Thomas "Number 10" walnut perpetual calendar shelf clock w/applied & turned decorations. Provisions for the date, day, & month are on the lower round tablet, eight-day time & strike, weight driven, 36" h. $4,000.

Ansonia carriage clocks; left, has elliptical dial, 30-hour, time only, 2 1/2 x 6" h. $600. Right, "Oriole" enameled in colors, w/brass framework, 30-hour, time & alarm, 6 1/2" h. $550.

CRYSTAL REGULATOR CLOCK

Crystal regulators are shelf clocks so named because they typically have clear glass panels on all four sides, allowing their works to be seen. They are also known for being precise timekeepers.

Ansonia "Regal" crystal regulator, finished in rich gold, visible (or open) escapement, mercury pendulum, beveled glass, eight-day, half-hour gong strike, 10 1/2 x 18 1/2" h. $4,500.

CUCKOO CLOCK

Cuckoo clocks, which originated in the Black Forest of Germany in the 1700s, are wall clocks that usually have ornately carved wooden cases in the shape of a house or cottage and are decorated with birds and foliage. On some models, when the clock strikes the hour, a bird pops out from behind a door, chirping the number of times that corresponds to the time.

GALLERY CLOCK

First introduced in 1845, gallery clocks have large round dials printed with large, dark numbers so they can be easily read from a distance. Thus, they were commonly used in train stations, lobbies, and other large public gathering places. They generally have plain cases with narrow borders to lend aesthetic balance to the oversized dials.

GRANDFATHER CLOCK

Grandfather clocks, also known as hall, tall, floor or long-case clocks, are weight-driven clocks first made in England in the 1660s. They were among the most common early clocks in the colonies because the settlers did not yet have mills capable of producing springs for spring-driven clocks. Grandfathers were large because they required a tall case to provide an adequate drop to run the clock. Those made in the colonies were copies of English styles.

Unknown maker, multi-colored wooden pendulette cuckoo clock, 30-hour, time only, spring-driven **$75**.

Seth Thomas oak gallery wall clock, 30-day, time only, ca. 1890, 24" d. **$750**.

Rich & Holt oak grandfather clock (American case, English movement), 30-hour, strikes hour on cast-iron bell, ca. 1920, 19" w. at top, 82" h. **$1,750**.

MANTEL CLOCK

Mantel clocks, otherwise known as shelf clocks, began replacing long-case (grandfather) clocks when spring-driven movements became available. Previously, clock cases were necessarily tall and bulky because weight-driven movements required a relatively long drop in order to operate. Mantel clocks also became more popular and affordable when mass-production methods were introduced.

METAL-FRONT CLOCK

Metal-front and metal-case clocks became more common in the U.S. after the mid-1850s as more foundries opened. Until then, wood had been the primary material for clock cases and works. Metal cases were commonly molded with elaborate designs and then painted or gilded.

MISSION-STYLE CLOCK

"Mission-style" refers to a plain design featuring oak in straight, sturdy lines. The style, also found in furniture, was popular from about 1900 to 1925.

MOTHER-OF-PEARL CASE CLOCK

In the mid-1800s, manufacturers began decorating clock cases with mother-of-pearl (pieces of the iridescent inner layer of certain mollusk shells) to create an Oriental look. The colorful pearly fragments were embedded in a layer of papier mâché, a mixture of mashed paper and glue.

Ansonia metal front mantel clock, gilded case, porcelain dial, eight-day time & strike, 7 1/2 x 10 1/2" h. **$275.**

Seth Thomas Plymouth Hollow cottage clock w/mother-of-pearl decorated case, eight-day time & strike, 11 x 17" h. **$450.**

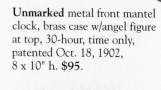

Unmarked metal front mantel clock, brass case w/angel figure at top, 30-hour, time only, patented Oct. 18, 1902, 8 x 10" h. **$95.**

Unknown maker, oak mission wall clock, exposed pendulum, 13 x 26" h. **$250.**

OAK SHELF CLOCK

Inexpensive oak kitchen clocks were produced in large numbers from the late 1800s to about 1915. Many had pressed designs created by a rotary press that forced the design into the wood after steam had softened it. The clocks commonly featured glass panels decorated with bronze or silver gilt.

OCTAGON CLOCK

Octagon clocks were often referred to as "schoolhouse clocks," but they were also used in large workplaces and factories to keep employees informed of the time. They are classified as short drop or long drop, depending on the length of the case. They were most common from the mid-1800s to the early 1900s.

OG (OGEE) CLOCK

An OG clock has an ogee, or S-shaped molding, around the door of its box frame and, usually, a decorated tablet. Early models were over two feet tall to accommodate their weight-driven movements. OGs were best sellers for nearly a hundred years, from 1825 to 1920.

PAPIER-MÂCHÉ CLOCK

Papier mâché clocks were introduced in the mid-1800s when manufacturers were experimenting with new designs. After mashed paper was mixed with glue and other adhesives, the easily molded product was pressed onto the clock, sometimes with added decorations such as mother-of-pearl. Later, manufacturers used a method of painting and gilding on cast-iron cases to create an imitation called "iron mâché."

W. L. Gilbert "Perfect" oak shelf clock, applied decorations & pressed designs, eight-day time, strike, & alarm, 15 x 23 1/2" h. **$350**.

Seth Thomas mahogany OG, eight-day time & strike, weight driven, 15 x 25" h. **$275**.

New Haven embossed oak simple calendar wall clock, eight-day time only, ca. 1910, 17 x 28" h. **$450**.

William S. Johnson, New York, black-enameled papier-mâché case w/mother-of-pearl inlay, eight-day time & strike w/winders below the dial, ca. 1895, 11 x 17" h. **$750**.

PARLOR CLOCK

Parlor clocks are products of the Victorian Era. Reflecting the formal style of this mid-to-late 1800s period, the clocks were elegant and intended to be displayed on a shelf or mantel in a family's parlor, typically the best room in the house, where guests were entertained. The clocks often have carved walnut cases and stenciled glass doors.

PORCELAIN CLOCK

Porcelain clocks have cases made of glazed ceramic. While the Royal Bonn Company of Germany made many of these colorful hand-painted cases, the Ansonia Clock Company made most of the works.

STATUE CLOCK

Figural clocks, now known as statue clocks, feature representations of people, animals, or mythical beings. Internationally, France was the most significant manufacturer of these clocks. Within the United States, the Ansonia Clock Company was the early leader.

Ansonia "Triumph" walnut parlor shelf clock, mirror sides w/cupid statues, applied metal decorations, eight-day time & strike, ca. 1890, 17 x 24" h. **$700**.

Ansonia Royal Bonn porcelain shelf clock w/open escapement, porcelain dial, eight-day time & strike, 13 1/2 x 15" h. **$1,400**.

New Haven statue clock w/cupid, gilded metal, 30-hour, time only, 5 x 6 1/2" h. **$350**.

STEEPLE CLOCK

In the 1840s, Elias Ingraham created this clock with a pointed Gothic-style "roof," two or four spires, and decorated glass tablet. The clocks used the newly developed brass springs and were tremendously popular; in fact, they are still made today.

TRIPLE-DECKER CLOCK

In the 1830s, during the American Empire Period, Elias Ingraham invented the three-deck, or triple-decker clock. Its tall case accommodated the drop needed for a weight-driven clock, as the springs required for a spring-driven clock could not yet be manufactured in the United States. Within fifteen years, smaller clock cases became more popular, and the production of triple-decker clocks began to wane.

E. N. Welch steeple shelf clocks; left, rosewood case, 30-hour, time, strike, & alarm, 8 x 15" h. **$250**.
Right, banded mahogany, 30-hour, time, strike, & alarm, ca. 1880, 10 x 19" h. **$200**.

C. & L. C. Ives Walnut triple-decker shelf clock, time & strike, weight driven, ca. 1830, 38" h. **$750**.

WALL REGULATOR CLOCK

A regulator is a clock with exceptional accuracy, made possible by the invention of the deadbeat escapement in 1715. Regulators were called such because they were used to regulate less accurate clocks and watches. For example, they were used in train stations and jewelry stores, where great accuracy was essential. Over time, however, less accurate clocks were labeled regulators, so eventually the term "regulator" just became a generic name for a hanging wall clock.

Seth Thomas "Regulator 6" oak wall clock, second hand, time only, brass weight & pendulum, ca. 1905, 16 x 48" h. **$2,400**.

Chapter 2
Clocks Through Time

The historical information and dates that follow present a succinct review of clock history. The information is as accurate as research permits; however, sources sometimes differ on dates, names, and other information.

Alfred the Great of England introduced the idea of using candles for clocks

1300s

1360	The first mechanical clock was constructed in France.
1380	Italy produced the first domestic clocks.
1386	England's earliest known public clock was installed at Salisbury Cathedral. It had no hands; instead, it indicated time by striking the hours.

1500s

1500	Peter Henlein of Nuremberg invented the mainspring.
1525	Jacob the Czech created the fusee.
1530	Screws for metal work became available.
Circa 1584	Galileo Galilei (1564-1642), an astronomer, physicist, and college professor born in Pisa, Italy, was credited with discovering the properties of the pendulum. Galileo was a twenty-year-old college student (slightly younger, according to some sources) when, on a visit to the city's cathedral, he watched a suspended lamp swinging back and forth. Timing it with the beat of his pulse, he discovered that a long swing moves faster than a short swing. Because of this quality, long and short swings take the same amount of time to make a complete cycle.

1600s

Early 1600s	Pendulums with anchor or deadbeat escapement replaced the less accurate foliot balance. Among the colonists who settled in 1607 and 1620 were skilled workers, including those with clockmaking knowledge. They made clocks one at a time, relying on England for their supplies.
1640	Germans began making Black Forest clocks.
Circa 1650	The first American tower clock was completed in Boston.
1657	Dutch scientist Christiaan Huygens created the first clock pendulum, based on Galileo's

observations. The pendulum's back and forth swinging motion served as the clock's regulating mechanism. This inventor's name is spelled in various ways by different authors. Most spell his first name with one "a," while his last name has appeared as Huijghens, Huygens, or Huyghens.

1660	The balance or hairspring came into use.
1673-1771	George Graham's two essential contributions to clockmaking were the deadbeat escapement and the mercurial compensation pendulum.
1680	Second hands made their first appearance.
Late 1600s	A London-made grandfather clock cost about $57. Its ebony or walnut case had fancy carving and gilded metal-applied decorations.

1700s

1700-1799	Clocks appeared in homes as a mark of prosperity.
1715	The deadbeat escapement was developed for regulator clocks.
1716	A public clock built by Joseph Phillips tolled the news of Washington's inauguration in New York City.
1721	George Graham's mercurial pendulum was first used.
1726	Ebenezer Parmelee of Guilford, Connecticut, built a clock that was installed in the town's church tower.
1727	John Harrison's gridiron pendulum was put into use.
1730	The German clockmaker Anton Ketterer made his first cuckoo clock.
1738-1770	In Lancaster, Pennsylvania, Abraham LeRoy made quality tall case clocks with brass dials. In colonial days, a few women were clockmakers. One of them, Anna Maria LeRoy, the daughter of Abraham LeRoy, watched her father at work and later produced clocks. She married Wilmer Atkinson in 1749. From 1750 to 1760, the dials of her clocks bore his name.
1740	The first cuckoo clocks were made in the Black Forest region of Germany, but several decades passed before they became popular.
After 1740	Mahogany was used for British clock cases.
1749-1796	David Rittenhouse became the most noted clockmaker in the Philadelphia area. In the years before the Revolutionary War, he inherited some books and tools from his uncle, which may have aroused his interest in mechanics. He began making high quality clocks in 1749. After the former English colonies became the United States of America, Rittenhouse met and began working with American leaders, including Benjamin Franklin and Thomas Jefferson. He made astronomical instruments and started the first

observatory in the United States, which gave him recognition as a scientist as well as a maker of quality clocks.

1750   Round dials were introduced for shelf clocks.

Edward Duffield made Philadelphia's first town clock.

1759   Thomas Mudge of London invented the lever escapement.

1760   The four Willard brothers from Grafton, Massachusetts, began learning clockmaking. Benjamin, the first to take up the trade, worked in various places, including Grafton. A clockmaker at that time could only produce twelve to twenty tall clocks a year. A hundred years later, about 150,000 shelf clocks were built a year. The great increase was due to the development of mass production.

1765   Pierre Le Roy of Paris invented the compensation balance.

1770   David Rittenhouse set up a clock shop in Philadelphia. His specialty was tall-case clocks with brass works.

1772-1852   Eli Terry became known as the father of the clockmaking industry.

Pre 1775   In colonial America, craftsmen made clocks to order, one at a time, which was an expensive process. They fashioned brass movements by hand with simple tools.

Boston, New York, and Philadelphia were all centers for the production of tall-case floor clocks, better known as grandfather clocks. By this time, several hundred clockmakers were at work in the colonies.

1775-1783   Clockmaking in the colonies came to a halt during the Revolutionary War as clockmakers joined the fighting forces or made equipment for soldiers. Many clockmakers became gunsmiths.

Circa 1789   Amos Jewett (1753-1834), a clockmaker in New Lebanon, New York, made wooden tall clocks with printed paper dials. He numbered and dated his clocks, so it can easily be determined that clock number twelve was made in 1789, while clock number thirty-eight was built in 1796.

1790 to 1812   Gideon Roberts, a Revolutionary War veteran, was possibly the first to use mass-production methods in his Bristol, Connecticut, clock factory, which produced both hanging wall clocks and tall-case floor clocks. Because brass clock works were expensive, he created his own wooden movements and used printed paper dials. Roberts assembled his thirty-hour, tall-case clocks in groups of ten or more at a time. This innovation accelerated production and made more affordable clocks available to buyers.

Some of Roberts' clocks were made without a case. The entire pendulum was visible as it swung back and forth, so the caseless clock earned the nickname "wag-on-the-wall clock." However, a buyer could build a case for it or hire a woodworker to make one to create a conventional clock.

1793	After Eli Terry completed his apprenticeship, he began making clocks near Plymouth, Connecticut.
Nov. 1797	Eli Terry was awarded a patent for an "equation clock," which had two dials. One dial showed sun time and the other true time.

1800s

Circa 1800	The production of wooden clocks began in the United States.
After 1800	Gideon Roberts owned an assembly plant in Richmond, Virginia.
	Eli Terry learned how to use water power to drive machinery. This helped to increase the production of clock parts.
1802-1840	Simon Willard made about four thousand clocks during this time. One model was the banjo clock, which sold for $35.
	Early nineteenth-century clockmaking was difficult because metal was scarce and the supply of glass was limited. All work had to be done by hand, and craftsmen and their apprentices used the simplest tools in their work: hammers, drills, and files.
1802	Simon Willard patented his "Improved Timepiece," later called the "banjo clock" because of its shape. Originally, most banjo clocks were time-only models. The popular banjo clock style has been copied consistently over the years.
	Eli Terry established his first factory.
1802-1860	Banjo clocks were made in the United States.
1806	Eli Terry was making about two hundred clocks a year.
1807-1809	The Jefferson Embargo limited importation of material from English factories.
1807-1810	Eli Terry contracted to make four thousand hang-up clock movements at $4 each in three years' time. This was an astonishing, unheard of quantity for his day. The waterpower-driven machines Terry designed produced identical interchangeable wooden parts for inexpensive (grandfather-type) clock works. While it's commonly believed that Henry Ford introduced the factory system of mass production, actually Terry is credited with developing this system nearly a hundred years earlier. As a result, he was able to produce large quantities of clocks, making inexpensive clocks available to the public.
	Silas Hoadley and Seth Thomas began their clockmaking careers working for Terry.
1809-1810	Eli Terry established a partnership with Seth Thomas.
1810	Seth Thomas and Silas Hoadley bought Eli Terry's Plymouth clock shop. Thomas sold his share of the shop to Hoadley in 1813.

1811-1830s	Six Ives brothers, including Joseph and Chauncey, became involved in the clock industry.
1812	Eli Terry opened an experimental shop that produced inexpensive wooden shelf clocks.
1813	Seth Thomas set up his own shop in Plymouth Hollow, Connecticut, where he became a prolific clockmaker.
1816	Eli Terry patented a pillar-and-scroll shelf clock with a thirty-hour wooden works that evolved from his plain box-type case. The clock cost about $15 and ran thirty hours on a single winding. For a short time, Chauncey Jerome made clock cases for Eli Terry.
August 1817	Joseph Ives (1782-1862) applied for a patent on "looking-glass" clock cases.
Circa 1818	Joseph Ives made a brass clock movement with steel plates.
	Seth Thomas and Eli Terry reached an agreement that Thomas was to pay Terry a royalty of fifty cents for each clock made. About five thousand clock movements were produced under the agreement.
July 1819	The firm of Joseph Ives and Company was dissolved.
1819-1822	Birge and his associates made large numbers of wall mirror clocks.
1820	Side-column clocks began to be manufactured.
1820-1830	Circumventing Terry's patent, other companies varied the pillar-and-scroll clock, frequently using brass eight-day movements.
1820-1840	Most of the Connecticut clock industry produced wooden shelf clocks. The clocks sold for less than $10. Brass clocks, on the other hand, ranged from $15 to $33 or more.
1822	Joseph Ives of Bristol patented a looking-glass clock, but Aaron Willard claimed that Massachusetts makers had been using looking glasses to add variety to clock fronts for some twenty-five years.
Circa 1822	The "lighthouse" clock was patterned after Eddystone Lighthouse in Plymouth, England, one of the earliest lighthouses in that country. Simon Willard introduced the clock, which was eight-day, weight-driven, and featured an alarm and a glass dome.
1822-1855	Birge was associated with the clockmakers Ives, Case, Gilbert, Fuller, and Peck.
1824	Chauncey Jerome formed a partnership with his brother, Noble, and with Elijah Darrow to manufacture clocks. They named the firm Jeromes & Darrow, which became the largest producer of clocks at the time.
	Joseph Ives perfected a spring-driven shelf clock using flat-leafed springs instead of coiled ones.
Circa 1825	Chauncey Jerome patented a bronze looking-glass clock with bronze-colored pilasters, a thirty-hour wooden movement, and a mirror instead of a tablet. Jerome specialized in

case building and usually bought his movements from others.

Joseph Ives learned how to make rolled brass. He moved to Brooklyn, New York, where he stayed briefly and invented the "wagon spring" to power clocks. The wagon spring is a series of flat-leafed arched springs that resemble those used on wagons.

1827	Chauncey Jerome invented a one-day, weight-driven clock named the "OG" (ogee), which sold for one dollar. OG clocks have veneer frames with S-curved molding.
1827-1920	OG clocks were widely made and sold throughout this ninety-three-year period. In fact, more than five hundred thousand sold in a single year.
1828	Elias Ingraham settled in Bristol, where he made cabinets and cases for clocks.
	Mark Leavenworth of Waterbury, Connecticut, made wooden movements for clocks.
After 1829	Samuel Terry (1774-1853) became an important producer of wooden movements in Bristol, Connecticut.
	Marsh, Gilbert & Company operated a clock business in Bristol.
1830	Eli Terry's son, Silas B. Terry, patented a method for tempering coiled springs so they could be produced inexpensively.
	Irenus Atkins, a Baptist minister, started a clock factory in Bristol, converting a church into a factory, as no other building was available for this purpose.
	The spring balance was invented.
After 1830	Rolled brass became more available for clock movements.
	Chauncey Jerome gave his brother, Noble, the idea for replacing wooden clock works with inexpensive rolled-brass movements. Some authorities believe Chauncey copied Joseph Ives' mirror clock and brass movement.
1831	Elias Ingraham founded the E. Ingraham Company.
	The Terrysville Post Office was established on December 22, 1831, in honor of Eli Terry.
	J. C. Brown made clocks in Bristol, Connecticut.
1831-1837	Burr & Chittenden was making clocks in Lexington, Massachusetts.
Circa 1832	Daniel Pratt, Jr., was a clockmaker in Reading, Massachusetts.
1832-1836	Relying on the combined resources of four factories, Boardman and Wells made a large number of wooden-movement shelf clocks.
1833	Elisha Brewster started a factory at Bristol under the name Brewster & Ingraham.
	Eli Terry retired from active clockmaking.
1836	James S. Ives of Bristol received a patent for a brass coiled clock spring.
1837-1843	Birge & Mallory experienced prosperity because of its volume of sales.

1838	The brass shelf clock was developed.
Circa 1840s	Elias Ingraham of Bristol designed the steeple clock, also known as the sharp Gothic clock.
1840	Spring-driven clocks were introduced.
	The largest clock factory was the Jerome Company, owned by Chauncey Jerome.
1840-1842	Chauncey Jerome sent a shipment of his brass clocks to England. When they arrived, the English authorities realized they were very inexpensive and reliable, so they allowed them to be sold. The buyers purchased the entire lot. When Jerome sent another lot, the buyers purchased all of them, too.
1840-1850	All American clocks were weight driven until the mid-nineteenth century because the United States did not have rolling mills that were capable of producing spring steel.
1842-1849	J. C. Brown became J. C. Brown & Company and also used the name Forestville Manufacturing Company.
	This period marked the partnership years of Edward Howard and David P. Davis, whose principal product was the banjo clock.
1843	The partnership of Boardman & Wells ended, and Wells and other clockmakers formed the Bristol Company.
1844	John Birge and Thomas Fuller formed a partnership that lasted until the death of Fuller in 1848.
	Brothers Elias and Andrew Ingraham formed a partnership with Elisha C. Brewster and started producing the steeple clock, which rapidly gained in popularity. This innovation soon replaced the large three-section Empire case, known as a "triple-decker," which had been a popular model among Connecticut clockmakers of the 1830s.
	Chauncey Jerome had twelve brass clock factories in Bristol and a case factory in New Haven, Connecticut.
1845	When one of Jerome's Bristol factories burned down, fifty to seventy-five thousand brass movements were destroyed.
	By this time, nearly a million clocks were being made each year in Connecticut.
1846	Chauncey Jerome moved his entire operation from Bristol to New Haven, Connecticut.
1847	An economic depression halted American clockmaking and led to the demise of the wooden clock movement.
1848	A Howard tower clock was installed in a church in New Hampshire.
1849	The American Clock Company, New York City, was organized as a large depository to

sell clocks made by various clockmakers. The company issued a catalog showing the clocks that were for sale.

1850	Weight-driven clocks were gradually replaced by spring-driven ones.
	Anson Phelps established the Ansonia Clock Company in Ansonia, Connecticut.
Circa 1850	Brass-coiled springs were largely replaced by better and cheaper steel springs.
	Nicholas Muller was working in a foundry in New York City, where he made iron-front clocks.
	Chauncey Jerome built America's largest clock manufacturing company.
1850-1860	Tall-clock production came to a standstill.
1851	Samuel Emerson Root was working in Bristol, where he made some marine-type movements.
Circa 1851	The William L. Gilbert Clock Company of Plymouth, Connecticut, was incorporated.
	Hiram Camp started the New Haven Clock Company in New Haven.
	John H. Hawes of Ithaca, New York, patented the first known simple-mechanism calendar clock.
After 1853	Many patents were issued for calendar clocks.
1853-1959	The New Haven Clock Company was in business.
1853-now	The Seth Thomas Clock Company was in business.
1854	A fire at the Ansonia Clock Company forced the company to move to Phelps Mill under the new name of the Ansonia Brass and Copper Company.
1855	The New Haven Clock Company took over the Jerome Manufacturing Company but continued to use the Jerome name.
	John Briggs of Concord, New Hampshire, received a patent for a clock escapement called the "Briggs Rotary."
	Ansonia patented the "bobbing doll" clock.
	The E. & A. Ingraham clock plant in Bristol burned.
	Chauncey Jerome went bankrupt because of financial reverses.
1855-1900+	Calendar clocks were popular during this time.
1857	The Waterbury Clock Company was in business.
	Solomon Spring owned a clock company.
1859	Ansonia patented its "swinging doll" clock.
	Seth Thomas died.
	Westminster chimes were introduced.
Circa 1863	F. Kroeber manufactured clocks in New York City, made fine cases, and often altered

purchased movements.

1863-1868	L. F. and W. W. Carter made calendar clocks.
1864	Mozart, Beach & Hubbell patented a perpetual-calendar clock that needed to be wound only once a year.
	E. N. Welch of Bristol consolidated the clock companies he purchased under the name of E. N. Welch Manufacturing Company.
1865	When the Ithaca Calendar Clock Company was established, it used Henry B. Horton's perpetual roller-type calendar clock patent.
	The American clock industry exported over $900,000 worth of clocks to over thirty countries.
1866	Plymouth Hollow was renamed Thomaston, Connecticut, to honor Seth Thomas.
1866-1964	The William L. Gilbert Clock Company was in business.
1867	A battery-operated clock was marketed.
	Alfonso Broadman, Forestville, Connecticut, made a simple calendar clock with two rollers, one for the month and the date, and the other for the day of the week.
1868	Welch, Spring & Company was organized, specializing in the manufacture of regulator and calendar clocks.
	Joseph K. Seem patented a method of attaching three small disks to the back of an existing clock dial, making it a simple calendar clock.
1868-1893	Parker & Whipple Clock Company operated in Meriden, Connecticut.
1869	Celluloid, a flammable plastic, was developed. It was later used on clock cases to simulate amber, onyx, tortoise shell, and other materials.
1870s-1880	George Owen of Winsted, Connecticut, owned a small shop that later merged with Gilbert and Company.
1871	Daniel Gale of Sheboygan, Wisconsin, patented an astronomical calendar clock dial.
1872	Terrysville, Connecticut, was renamed Terryville.
	Joseph K. Seem obtained a patent for a perpetual-calendar roller mechanism that could be fitted on top of an existing clock when space permitted.
1878 or before	Ansonia clocks were marked "Ansonia, Connecticut."
1878 or later	Ansonia clocks were marked "New York."
1879	The Ansonia Clock Company moved to Brooklyn, New York. Shortly after the move, a fire destroyed the factory.
Circa 1880	Nicholas Muller's Sons made fancy shelf-clock cases of iron and bronze.
	The lyrics of a song gave the long-case clock its nickname: "My grandfather clock was

too tall for the shelf, so it stood ninety years on the floor." Since this time, the long-case clock has been known as the grandfather clock.

1880 — H. J. Davis made an illuminated alarm clock.

1881 — Joseph K. Seem was granted a patent that improved his original 1872 perpetual-calendar mechanism.

1881-1885 — Yale Clock Company, New Haven, Connecticut, advertised novelty clocks.

1882 — The Macomb Calendar Clock Company was formed in Illinois. The company used Seem's 1881 calendar clock patent.

1883 — The Macomb Calendar Clock Company went out of business.

A. D. Clausen patented the "Ignatz" or "Flying Pendulum" clock.

Benjamin Franklin of Chicago patented a perpetual calendar clock mechanism that could be attached to an existing clock by cutting a hole in its dial.

1885 — The Sidney Advertising Clock Company of Sidney, New York, developed a large wall clock on which advertising drums turned every five minutes.

1885 — The United Clock Company was formed and made about fifty alarm clocks a day. The company only lasted two years, however, before going bankrupt.

1886-1916 — The Darche Electric Clock Company of Chicago, Illinois, and Jersey City, New Jersey, made battery-alarm timepieces.

1888 — The F. Kroeber Clock Company catalogue showed a selection of eight-day walnut shelf or mantel clocks with gong strike. The models were named Fulton, Angel Swing No. 2, Corinth, Congress, Mariposa, Leghorn, Jefferson, Floretta, Essex, Virgil, Wanderer, Vixen, Thunderer, Polaris, Arctic, and Langtry.

Circa 1888 — The Self Winding Clock Company of New York City made electric and battery-powered clocks.

1890 — Edward P. Baird & Company was established in Plattsburgh, New York. Its clocks used Seth Thomas works and had papier-mâché bodies.

Circa 1890 — The Jenning Brothers Manufacturing Company of Bridgeport, Connecticut, made metal clocks.

1891-1897 — Henry Prentiss of New York City received various patents for calendar mechanisms that ran for a year on a single winding.

1893 — The Parker Clock Company of Meriden, Connecticut, took over Parker & Whipple. The firm made novelty clocks, round alarm clocks, and small pendulum desk clocks.

1895 — The Western Clock Manufacturing Company began in La Salle, Illinois.

1896-1900 — Edward P. Baird & Company moved to Evanston, Illinois, where it made wooden-case clocks with metal dials trimmed with embossed and painted advertisements.

1897	The Chelsea Clock Company operated in Chelsea, Massachusetts. The company's output included automobile and ship clocks, as well as those for the home.
Late 1800s	The Simplex Company of Gardner, Massachusetts, made time recorders and time clocks. Decalcomania transfers were common on clock tablets.

1900s

1902	John P. Peatfield of Arlington, Massachusetts, patented a perpetual-calendar clock with a spring-driven mechanism that was wound yearly.
1903	The Sessions Clock Company of Bristol-Forestville, Connecticut, bought the E. N. Welch Manufacturing Company.
1903-1968	The Sessions Clock Company was in business.
1908	The Loheide Manufacturing Company made a black-case, metal-trimmed shelf clock containing a slot-machine device that accepted $2.50 gold pieces. The patent number 883,886 dates the clock to 1908.
1910	Big Ben alarm clocks were made.
1915	Little Ben alarm clocks were made.
Circa 1917	Paul Lux of Waterbury, Connecticut, founded the Lux Clock Manufacturing Company and produced many novelty clocks. He used molded wood cases.
1929	The Soviet government purchased the Ansonia Clock Company's equipment and materials and moved them to the Soviet Union.
1931	August C. Keebler of Chicago founded the August C. Keebler Company, which marketed Lux Clocks, including the pendulettes that he sold to large mail-order companies. He did not make clocks, but his name was sometimes used on Lux Clocks.
	Westclox, a trade name, became the new name for Western Clock Manufacturing Company.

Chapter 3
Histories of Clock Manufacturers

Leading Manufacturers

The Ansonia Clock Company

Anson G. Phelps, a wealthy Connecticut importer of tin, brass, and copper, founded the Ansonia Clock Company in 1850, six years after he built a copper rolling mill near Derby, Connecticut. Phelps started the business with $100,000. He and his associates, Eli Terry and Franklin C. Andrews, advertised their firm in the Connecticut Business Directory with the following statement: "Ansonia Clock Company, Manufacturers and Dealers in Clocks and Timepieces of Every Description, Wholesale and Retail, Ansonia, Connecticut."

After a fire destroyed the factory in 1854, Phelps' company moved to Ansonia, where it was renamed the Ansonia Brass and Copper Company. The company made clocks there from 1854 to 1878. When it moved its clockmaking operations to Brooklyn, New York in 1878, it was reorganized under its original name: the Ansonia Clock Company. In 1879, shortly after

Ansonia "La Charny" Royal Bonn porcelain shelf clock, porcelain dial, French sash bezel, eight-day time & strike, 11 x 12" h. **$675**.

this move, a fire destroyed the factory. A year later, after completing a new factory in Brooklyn, Ansonia expanded its business. The company developed many new styles of clocks, and novelty and figurine clocks became a big part of its enterprise.

Ansonia introduced all sorts of wall and shelf clocks, including swing clocks. The company marketed imitation French clocks as well as novelties, such as the "Bobbing Doll" and "Swinging Doll," which it patented in 1855 and 1859 respectively. An 1889 catalog of Ansonia clocks featured three versions of the Bobbers, called Jumper No. 1, Jumper No. 2, and Jumper No. 3. Ansonia was known for its diversity of clock types; many of the older and unusual ones have been reproduced, including the "Bobbing" and "Swinging" dolls.

The company's specialty clocks included the swing clocks, in which female figures held swinging pendulums. Also popular were the Royal Bonn porcelain shelf varieties and the statue clocks, which the company advertised as figure clocks. Among its novelty clocks, the Crystal Palace, Sonnet, Helmsmen, and Army and Navy clocks have proved to be excellent collector's items and have rapidly increased in value. The clocks were marked "New York" as their place of origin.

Just prior to World War I, Ansonia had sales representatives in Australia, New Zealand, Japan, China, India, and a score of other countries. After the conclusion of the war, its business deteriorated in quality and dropped significantly in the number of clocks produced. Manufacturing stopped in the spring of 1929. By the end of that year, the company's material assets were sold to the Russian government. Sad as it was to accept, this great clock manufacturing company, as creative as any other American clock company, was defunct after the summer of 1929.

The William L. Gilbert Clock Company

George Marsh and William Lewis Gilbert purchased a clock shop in 1828, which they named Marsh, Gilbert & Company. They were soon at work in two Connecticut cities, Bristol and Farmington.

In 1837, when John Birge joined Gilbert, the company name became Birge, Gilbert & Company. They made Empire-style shelf clocks.

The company name continued to change. From 1839 to 1840, the company was known as Jerome, Grant, Gilbert & Company. Clockmakers Zelotas Grant, and Chauncey and Noble Jerome became partners with Gilbert to create Jerome's inexpensive brass movement clocks.

In 1841, Gilbert and Lucius Clarke acquired a clock factory in Winsted, Connecticut. Later the town name was changed to Winchester. Ezra Baldwin was a member of this company for a time.

From 1841 to 1845 Clarke, Gilbert & Company produced inexpensive brass clocks. In 1845 William Lewis Gilbert purchased Clarke's share in the company, but three years later, Clarke bought his shares back. The partnership lasted until 1851. The company name became W. L. Gilbert & Company until 1866, when the Gilbert Manufacturing Company was established. In 1871, the Winsted (or Winchester) factory burned down. Gilbert was not a quitter; he formed the William L. Gilbert Clock Company that very same year. Gilbert died in 1890, but the company name was retained for sixty-three years.

W. L. Gilbert
mahogany OG, eight-day time & strike, weight driven, 15 1/2 x 26" h. $250.

George B. Owen managed the company from 1880 to about 1900. Despite financial problems from 1934 to 1957, the company remained active as the William L. Gilbert Clock Corporation.

During World War II, clock production was limited because the war effort required metal. The clock company was allowed to manufacture papier-mâché case alarm clocks rather than metal ones. The clocks enabled workers to get to their war-related jobs on time.

After the General Computing Company took over the Gilbert Company, the new owners used the name General-Gilbert Corporation.

By 1964, the company clock division was no longer profitable. Spartus Corporation of Chicago and Louisville, Mississippi, purchased the company.

The E. Ingraham Company

Elias Ingraham (1805-1885) founded the E. Ingraham Company. He served a five-year apprenticeship with Daniel Dewey as a cabinet-maker. In 1828 he went to work for George Mitchell, a wise businessman in Bristol, Connecticut. Mitchell wanted a worker who was creative and could produce new case styles. By succeeding in this task, Ingraham earned the reputation of being an innovative man in the clock industry. The exotic case he designed had mahogany columns, paw feet, turned rosettes, and carved baskets of fruit.

In 1830 Ingraham went to work for Chauncey and Lawson C. Ives to design cases for their clocks. One of his cases, which could accommodate a long drop of weights, was a triple-decker. In the three years that followed, Ingraham made almost six thousand cases for Chauncey and Lawson C. Ives.

During the next ten years, Ingraham made clock cases, chairs, and mirrors. He helped design a Gothic case, named a steeple clock, which became extremely popular. These smaller clocks rapidly replaced the large Empire-style cases.

In the mid-1840s, he formed a partnership called Brewster and Ingraham. Members of the clockmaking company were Elisha Brewster and the Ingraham brothers, Elias and Andrew. The Ingraham Company, with its various name changes and partners, became one of the world's largest clockmakers.

E. Ingraham oak kitchenette shelf clock, eight-day time & strike, ca. 1930, 13 1/2 x 13 1/2"h. **$150**

The following advertisement is taken verbatim from a Brewster & Ingraham promotional public notice:

BREWSTER & INGRAHAMS

Have constantly on hand, at their FACTORY,

in Bristol, Conn.,

Their various Styles of Patent Spring

Eight Day and Thirty Hour

Brass Clocks,

In Mahogany, Zebra, Rosewood and

Black-Walnut Cases.

Also Gallery, Hall and Counting-House

Eight Day Time-Pieces of

10 Inches to 22 Inches in diameter, in Gilt,

Mahogany and Black Walnut Cases.

ALSO AN IMPROVED KIND OF

EIGHT DAY AND THIRTY HOUR

MARINE TIME-PIECES,

All which are made in the best manner.

The Proprietors are constantly present to

attend to all orders, whether large or small,

at as low prices, regard being had to quality,

as at any other Factory in the country.

THEY HAVE ALSO A HOUSE AT

NO. 13 WALBROOK, CITY LONDON,

ENGLAND.

Where they keep constantly on hand a large

assortment of the above kinds of

Clocks, together with Eight Day and

Thirty Hour OG WEIGHT CLOCKS.

Please call and examine before

purchasing elsewhere.

E. C. Brewster. E. Ingraham. A. Ingraham

In 1855, the Ingraham factory in Bristol burned, resulting in a loss of about $30,000. Elias Ingraham formed a new company when he made his son Edward a partner in 1857. They used the name E. Ingraham & Company from 1861 to 1880. In 1881, they added the word "The" to the name to make it The E. Ingraham & Company. This name stayed as such until 1884, when "&" was dropped to make it simply, The E. Ingraham Company. During this period, the company manufactured clocks with black-painted or japanned cases. Over two hundred different models were built.

From 1914 to 1942, some of the company's products included non-jeweled pocket watches, wrist watches, eight-day lever movement clocks, electric clocks, and pendulum clocks.

When the company was sold to McGraw-Edison in 1967, clockmaking ceased in Bristol.

The New Haven Clock Company

In the early 1850s, the New Haven Clock Company was incorporated with $20,000. The president of the company was Hiram Camp, who retained that title for forty years.

The company was formed to produce inexpensive brass movements for the Jerome Manufacturing Company, but the Jerome company went bankrupt and had to sell its assets, including its manufacturing plant. Good fortune arose when the New Haven Clock Company purchased the defunct Jerome Company. From that day in the mid-1850s, until the 1880s, the company experienced great success. In addition to expanding its operations by making complete clocks, it promoted pocket watches and wrist watches.

New Haven soon became one of the largest clock companies in the United States. Among the clocks produced were French clocks; jewelers' regulators; ebony and mahogany cabinet clocks; wall clocks (including calendar varieties); figure clocks (now called statue clocks); and tall-case hall clocks.

New Haven sales offices were located around the world in such cities as Liverpool, England; and Yokohama, Japan. Through catalogs, New Haven sold its own clocks, as well as those made by F. Kroeber of New York, the E. Howard Company of Boston, and E. Ingraham & Company of Bristol. New Haven discontinued this sales practice in 1885, however. After that, the firm offered only a small number of imported clocks and no longer sold any clocks manufactured by other companies.

A novelty clock, the "Flying Pendulum" was patented in the early 1880s. The New Haven Clock Company took control of the patent and improved

New Haven statue clock of standing cupid figure, bronze & brass, 4 1/2 x 6 1/2" h. $150.

its mechanism and design. Its unique movement makes it one of the most fascinating clocks ever produced. A flying ball attached to a swiveling center pole alternately wraps and unwraps around two side poles, regulating the movement and taking the place of the pendulum. The Flying Pendulum clock was advertised as the best show-window attraction ever made, but it was not noted for its timekeeping accuracy. This unique clock has been reproduced from time to time, and as recently as the late 1950s.

In 1910, the company offered a vast range of clocks and from 1917 to 1956, the clockmaker was a major producer of inexpensive watches. A corporation, The New Haven Clock and Watch Company, took over the company in 1946. Financial woes plagued New Haven from 1956 to 1959. After 107 years in business, the New Haven Clock Company's facilities and products were sold at a public auction in March 1960. One reason for the company's demise was its tremendous overproduction of products, which made it impossible to earn a profit.

The Seth Thomas Clock Company

Seth Thomas (1786-1859) became an apprentice in the cabinetmaker-joiner trade in the early 1800s. He worked with Silas Hoadley around 1808 to 1810, under the supervision of Eli Terry near Waterbury, Connecticut. Eli Terry needed help to fulfill a contract for four thousand wooden hang-up clocks, including their movements, pendulums, dials, and hands. Thomas, as a joiner, assembled the clocks using his woodworking techniques. All clocks were in running order when he finished.

In 1810, Seth Thomas and Silas Hoadley bought Eli Terry's plant. They made tall-case clocks and thirty-hour clocks with wooden movements. In 1813, Seth Thomas sold his share of the business to Silas Hoadley and bought a shop in Plymouth Hollow, Connecticut, where he made tall-case clocks with wooden movements. This shop remained his workplace until 1853.

In 1839, Seth Thomas changed from using wooden to thirty-hour brass clock movements, and in about 1850 he began using springs instead of

Seth Thomas "18 Inch Lobby" oak wall clock, second hand, incised carving, lever movement, 15-day, time only, 25 x 38" h. $2,500.

weights to power his clocks.

Thomas, who was primarily known for clockmaking, was also known as a good businessman. He diversified his financial interests and acquired a considerable amount of farmland. In the early 1800s at the age 48, he bought a cotton factory, which he operated profitably until the Civil War began in 1861. By 1844, he had stopped making wooden clocks. As a traditionalist he was reluctant to change his clockmaking methods, but producing brass clocks was more profitable. Thomas' company was soon producing twenty thousand brass clocks annually. At the height of his brass clock production, he built a brass rolling mill called the Thomas Manufacturing Company.

From 1853 to 1865, the Seth Thomas Clock Company operated in Plymouth Hollow. After Thomas' death in 1859, his three sons—Aaron, Edward, and Seth Junior—carried on the business, creating many new models of spring-driven clocks. In addition, calendar clocks became an important part of their line.

The residents of Plymouth Hollow respected Seth Thomas for the industries he established in the town. To show their appreciation, the town was renamed Thomaston six years after his death.

In the 1880s, the Seth Thomas Clock Company employed about 825 people. Over seventy of them were children. The workers put in a ten-hour workday and were paid from $1.50 to $3.00 a day. Skilled mechanics were at the top of the pay scale, while laborers were at the bottom. With this staff, the company produced approximately $729,000 in clocks annually.

The Seth Thomas Company, in the hands of family members, remained a success. It holds the distinction of being the longest established American clockmaking company. Seth Thomas profited from his leadership ability, becoming one of the wealthiest men in Connecticut by the time he died in 1859.

In 1879, the Seth Thomas Clock Company and Seth Thomas Sons & Company consolidated. In 1931 the Seth Thomas Clock Company became a division of General Time Corporation. Seth Thomas' great-grandson, Seth E. Thomas Jr., was chairman of the board until his death in 1932. The company's leadership then passed out of the family's hands and in 1970 became a division of Talley Industries.

Waterbury cast-iron black enameled mantel clock, porcelain & brass dial, brass applied decorations, eight-day time & strike, 10 x 11" h. $300.

The Waterbury Clock Company

The Waterbury Clock Company was a major clock producer in the United States from 1857 to 1944—almost ninety years. It was originally begun as a branch of the Benedict & Burnham Manufacturing Company, the largest brass producer in Waterbury. The company manufactured rolled and drawn brass, copper, cabinet hardware, and lamp burners.

Waterbury was located in the Benedict & Burnham shops until it moved to larger quarters in Waterbury, Connecticut. It grew so rapidly that by 1873 it had expanded several times. By the late 1800s, Waterbury employed about three thousand people and made over twenty thousand watches and clocks daily. Waterbury became internationally known in the 1870s when it had offices in Toronto, Canada; and Glasgow, Scotland.

Waterbury made and sold movements as well as complete clocks. By the turn of the century, it had a business relationship with Sears Roebuck, one of the big mail-order houses. Waterbury sold many styles of clocks, including eight-day time & strike models in oak cases, which sold for $2 each.

In 1913, a Waterbury factory catalog illustrated

over four hundred styles of clocks, starting at $1.20 each. Included were alarm, carriage, French mantel, and tall clocks. In the early 1890s, the firm manufactured non-jeweled watches, including the famous dollar watch made for R. H. Ingersoll & Bros., and acted as selling agents for the Ithaca Calendar Clock Company. This latter affiliation lasted until 1891, when Waterbury introduced its own line of perpetual-calendar clocks.

During the Depression of the 1930s, the company went into receivership, and its case shop and clockmaking materials and parts were sold at auction. Waterbury's life as a clock and watch manufacturer ended when United States Time Corporation bought the company in 1944.

The E. N. Welch Manufacturing Company

Prior to 1831, Elisha Niles Welch (1809-1887) was in business with his father, George, who operated an iron foundry in Bristol. The foundry made weights and bells for clocks. When Elisha Welch formed a partnership with Thomas Barnes Jr., they named the company Barnes & Welch. The firm manufactured wooden-movement shelf clocks and was involved in business with

E. N. Welch
mahogany miniature OG, 30-hour, time & strike, original dial & tablet, 12 x 19" h. **$225**.

Jonathan C. Brown and Chauncey Pomeroy.

From 1841 to 1849, E. N. Welch partnered with J. C. Brown, who used Forestville Manufacturing Company and J. C. Brown, Bristol, Connecticut, as company names. Chauncey Pomeroy was also a partner in these companies. The two factories manufactured eight-day clocks with brass movements.

In 1853, fire destroyed J. C. Brown's Forestville Hardware and Clock Company.

Welch bought Elisha Manross' failing clock parts business and J. C. Brown's Forestville company after it went bankrupt. He also purchased Frederick S. Otis' casemaking business. He consolidated these purchases under one name, E. N. Welch, which became one of Bristol's largest clock companies. In 1868, the Welch, Spring & Company was formed. It emphasized high-quality clocks, including regulators and calendars. After Elisha Welch's death in 1887, his son James became the company's president.

Unfortunately, fire destroyed the movement factory in 1899. Later that same year, the case factory met the same fate. As a result, financial problems plagued the company. Mortgages were past due and bank notes were due and unpaid. Liabilities were growing and legal suits were pending. Realizing the troubles that faced the Welch clockmakers, the Sessions family, who had a clock business in Forestville and were interested in expanding their business, began buying Welch company stock. After Albert L. Sessions became treasurer and W. E. Sessions assumed the presidency, they borrowed over $50,000 to revitalize the company. At this time, the Welch Company ceased to exist, and the name was changed to the Sessions Clock Company.

The Welch, Spring & Company

The Welch, Spring & Company was organized by three clock enthusiasts—Elisha Niles Welch, Solomon Crosby Spring, and Benjamin Bennet Lewis. Their partnership lasted for sixteen years, from 1868 to 1884.

Each of these men brought a talent that contributed to the success of the organization. Welch was the financier, Spring was the manager and design engineer, and Lewis was the inventor. These men were interested in developing a superior clock line, in contrast to most other American clock companies at the time, which sought quantity rather than quality.

Welch, Spring & Co. rosewood calendar clock w/B. B. Lewis' perpetual movement, patented Dec. 18, 1868, eight-day time & strike, 11 x 20" h. **$1,050.**

At 22, Welch formed a partnership with Thomas Barnes using a Barnes and Welch label as the company's logo. On two separate occasions, in 1841 and again in 1880, Welch loaned money to J. C. Brown, a fellow clockmaker. When Brown's company became insolvent, Welch purchased it from him and bought two other Bristol firms—The Forestville Hardware and Clock Company and The Frederick Otis Case Shop. He consolidated these clock holdings under the name of E. N. Welch Manufacturing Company. Because he was a wise and cautious investor, he was consistently successful in business. In fact, it was largely due to Welch's support that the Welch, Spring & Co. succeeded.

Lewis' contribution to the new company was his ability to develop calendar mechanisms. He received three patents for perpetual-calendar mechanisms, dated 1862, 1864, and 1868.

The remaining member of the company, Spring, was a renowned casemaker who specialized in rosewood cases. He learned basic techniques while working for the Atkins Clock Company. After leaving this company, he spent about twenty years operating his own business. After purchasing the defunct Birge, Peck & Company, he named it the

S. C. Spring Clock Company. The newly reorganized company supplied cases, movements, and parts to clockmakers in the Bristol, Connecticut, area. He also manufactured vast numbers of clocks for the parent company.

Welch, Spring & Company passed through four stages during its sixteen years. The first stage, from 1868 to 1869, was devoted to creating a standard shelf model. The company produced three models—the Empress, the Peerless, and the Italian.

During the second stage, lasting from 1870 to 1876, emphasis was on the production of regulators and calendar clocks. Only five styles of regulators and five styles of calendars were made. All of the calendar clocks used the B. B. Lewis perpetual-calendar mechanism and could be purchased with walnut or rosewood cases. The majority of the No. 1 regulators were made with rosewood cases. The walnut case, at $95, was too expensive for the average American, so few were produced in this model.

In the third stage, from 1877 to 1888, the company focused on selecting clock names that were familiar to the public and that implied quality. Other manufacturers were naming their clocks after regents, cities, and rivers, so Spring and other staff members decided to name their series after popular opera and theater stars of the day. The 1877 Spring models included the names of seven composers and opera singers—Parepa, Lucca, Titiens, Verdi, Kellogg, Auber, and Wagner.

The names were used for a variety of clock styles, including shelf clocks, regulators, octagons, and calendar clocks. The two shelf clocks available in rosewood were the Parepa and the Lucca. The latter was also made as a regulator, and the Titiens, a shelf clock, was made with a walnut case. The octagon clock was dubbed the Verdi, and the wall regulator in walnut was named the Kellogg. The other two—the Auber, a shelf calendar clock, and the Wagner, in both wall and shelf calendar versions—had black walnut cases.

The fourth and final stage, called the Patti Era, lasted for five years, from 1879 to 1884. This developmental period was named for Adelina Patti (1843-1919), a Spanish coloratura soprano who won fame as one of the world's greatest operatic singers. Her career was almost without parallel in the history of opera.

This period marked the company's final effort to be financially successful. The staff believed the company's success would depend on the success of the Patti model. The original Patti clock was known for its fancy column turnings, glass sides, rosettes, and fancy finials. Its case was rosewood and featured a Sandwich glass pendulum. The Patti was considered by many as the most collectible and famous parlor clock ever conceived by an American manufacturer. However, sales did not live up to expectations.

The company tried to dress up the Patti to improve its sales. It added French-style cloverleaf hands, a brass pendulum with a Sandwich glass center, a gold leaf border on the glass door panel, and a bell mounted on the movement. Black labels with gold print replaced the white labels with black print.

These changes, however, did not solve the

company's problem. The Welch, Spring, & Company failed because the clocks were too costly to produce and too expensive for the public to buy. In 1884, the company ceased doing business. E. N. Welch purchased all the buildings, inventory, and machinery of the Welch, Spring & Company for $10,000. Mass production had won, and the ornate "Patti" clocks failed to appeal to the average citizen because of their high cost. Despite this, E. N. Welch died a wealthy man in 1887, leaving an estate of approximately three million dollars.

Smaller Clock Manufacturers

E. Howard Clock Company

In the early 1800s, Edward Howard (1813-1904) served as an apprentice clockmaker under the supervision of Aaron Willard Jr., while David P. Davis served as a fellow apprentice.

After completing their apprenticeships, Howard and Davis formed a partnership with Luther Stephenson. They opened the firm Stephenson, Howard & Davis in Boston and practiced their trade until the mid-1840s. Although Stephenson left the company, the remaining two partners carried on the business until the late 1850s. Then, Davis

E. Howard & Co. oak railroad regulator wall clock, 17 x 64" h. $8,500.

also quit, leaving Howard alone in the reorganized E. Howard & Company in Roxbury, Massachusetts.

Howard made banjo, regulator, and turret clocks. His reputation as a manufacturer of high quality clocks with high prices has kept his clocks in the "highly sought after" category. Some of his astronomical regulators are priced at $15,000 or more. Howard's sidewalk or post clocks are especially rare and costly and are probably all in the hands of private collectors. As a result, they are almost never seen at public auctions or sales. If you find a Howard Clock and purchase it, keep it as is, rather than refinishing it. The clock will lose value if its finish is changed.

In 1958, the company stopped producing clocks, with the exception of tower clocks, which it continued to make until 1964.

Ithaca Calendar Clock Company

The Ithaca Calendar Clock Company was established in 1865 using Henry Bishop Horton's perpetual roller-type calendar clock patent. Horton (1819-1885) was granted two calendar clock patents, the first on April 18, 1865. The second, issued on August 28, 1866, was an improvement on his first patent. Because Horton's clock was a perpetual-calendar clock, it could be adjusted to automatically compensate for a leap year.

From about 1855, until the turn of the

century, calendar clocks were very popular, and larger companies manufactured several models of them. Most calendar clocks used a simple mechanism that required corrections to be made to accommodate leap year and the irregular number of days in the months. With the perpetual calendar device, however, no manual changes had to be made for the entire year.

Ithaca specialized in calendar clocks, but Horton could not find manufacturers in the Connecticut area who would use his mechanism in their clocks. He was independent enough, however, to establish a factory in Ithaca, New York, where the cases and calendar mechanisms were made.

The clock faces on the Ithaca clocks had two circular dials, one above the other. The top dial indicated the time, while the bottom dial showed the day of the week, the date of the month, and the month of the year. In most cases, the two dials have the same diameter, but in some clocks, the top dial is smaller than the bottom one.

These unique clocks were shipped to various parts of the world and were available in fifteen languages. Most ran for eight days, although some were thirty-day clocks. Walnut, rosewood, and painted cases were available.

Unfortunately, in 1876 a fire destroyed the Ithaca clock factory. Destructive fires were common occurrences among clock companies. Undaunted, Henry Horton secured another building and business continued as usual, but the business began to decline after 1900 and finally went bankrupt. Today perpetual calendar clocks are extremely expensive. Prices can soar to $4,000 or more.

The instruction label that follows was found on the outside of the back of an Ithaca calendar clock. We print it here to show you how exacting a company can be about its product.

Ithaca Calendar Clock Company, "Farmers" walnut perpetual calendar shelf clock, w/Welch movement & provisions for the date, day, & month on the lower tablet, eight-day time & strike, ca. 1865, 25 1/2" h. **$750**.

ITHACA CALENDAR CLOCK CO.
Ithaca, N. Y.

DIRECTIONS

The pendulum Ball and Key will be found

fastened either at the

bottom or top of the clock

The time now stands at 5 minutes

before 11 P.M.

If the clock is to be set IN THE MORNING,

turn the minute hand forward

until the right hour is reached.

If the clock is to be set IN THE

AFTERNOON, turn the minute

hand forward through TWELVE HOURS

and then to the right hour.

The calendar changes at midnight.

Set the clock in position and attach

the pendulum ball.

The clock must be perpendicular to insure

a perfect beat.

NEVER MOVE THE HOUR HAND by itself,

as the calendar would not change at the proper hour.

TO SET THE CALENDAR - Raise the wire on

the top of the clock and turn the calendar hand forward

(never backward) until the right

month and day of month is shown.

Still holding up the wire turn the day of the week

UPWARD till right.

CAUTION — USE NO OIL ON THE

CALENDAR. It is not needed, and

will work only injury when used by attracting dust

and clogging the machine.

TO REGULATE THE TIME — Raise or lower

the pendulum all by means of the nut below it.

If the clock does not strike correctly, raise the small

wire at the left under the seat on which rests the time

movement, and repeat until it strikes correctly. But this

cannot be done within 15 minutes of the striking hour.

This clock strikes the half hours.

THE BEST TIME TO CORRECT THE

STRIKE IS IMMEDIATELY AFTER THE

HOUR IS STRUCK.

This Clock is set for 19___

Every clock before leaving the works is tested

thoroughly, both as to time and Calendar,

and the Calendar being set on the right year

when the clock is packed,

will give the Leap year and other Februarys

correctly unless interfered with,

or worked ahead of time.

But if this should occur, it can readily be set

right as follows: Raise the wire as above, turn the

pointer forward until a February is shown, and

then place the pointer on the Figure 29,

drop the wire and if the pointer cannot be moved

you have a Leap Year February.

If the pointer is not holding fast on the figure 29,

continue the process until it is.

Calling this the Last Leap Year,

work forward as before

to the right year and month.

No women or children are employed in these works.

Joseph Ives

Joseph Ives (1782-1862) of Connecticut was an inventor and clockmaker. Wooden clock movements were in vogue when Joseph entered the clock trade. He followed this trend and fashioned wooden movements. Soon, however, he realized brass movements would be better, especially those made from rolled sheet brass, so he developed a rolling pinion, a small gear with teeth that fit into those of a larger gear or rack. Normally, a rolling pinion has fewer than twenty teeth called leaves.

In addition, Ives patented a steel spring. He is credited with a possible American first when he developed this successful clock spring. Until then, only English clockmakers had made and used steel springs successfully.

He headed Joseph Ives & Company of Bristol, Connecticut, from 1818 to 1819. Sometime later, Ives was credited with inventing the wagon-spring clock. He used these flat springs that resembled the flat leaf springs on a wagon to power clock movements. Around 1826, Ives moved to Brooklyn, New York, and for about five years made wagon-spring clocks. He served as a guiding light for the Ives business until his death in 1862.

Among Ives' clock creations is the "Duncan Phyfe" or "Brooklyn"-type wagon-spring clock. The dial on this clock is decorated with a vase of flowers and a painted picture on the tablet. He also developed a thirty-day, wagon-spring, time-only clock, in which the winding holes were positioned near 2 and 10 on the dial, rather than next to the 4 and 8, as on most clocks. Other Ives clocks include a thirty-day wagon-spring clock `in a drop octagon

case; a "Connecticut Lyre" eight-day wall clock with a gold-leaf front decoration; and a one-day wagon-spring hourglass clock with a label that read "Plainville, Conn."

Joseph was the most well known of six brothers involved in clockmaking. His five brothers also contributed significantly to the industry. Their names are as follows: Ira (1775-1848), Amasa (1777-1817), Philo (1780-1822), Shaylor (1785-1840), and Chauncey (1787-1857). It is possible that the Ives brothers inherited their interest in clocks from their father, Amas Ives of Bristol, who worked from 1770 to 1790.

One author said that these brothers gained fame when they became an integral part of Bristol clock history. Amazingly, they were issued a total of eleven patents on clocks. Ira received two—one for a time-and-strike clock and another for pinions. Shaylor had two patents for clock springs, and Joseph earned seven. All were a credit to their profession and each produced quality clocks.

F. Kroeber Clock Company

In the minds of clock collectors, the name F. Kroeber Clock Company conjures up images of expensive clocks rarely available to the average buyer. The maker of these clocks was Florence Kroeber (1840-1911), who was born in Germany in 1840. He and his family immigrated to the United States in the mid-1800s and settled in New York City.

At 19, Kroeber was employed as a bookkeeper in the Owen and Clark Clock Store. George B. Owen operated the business when Clark left the company in 1861. Soon, George B. Owen left to become general manager of the W. L. Gilbert Clock Company in Winsted, Connecticut, which gave Kroeber the opportunity to acquire the business. Kroeber then offered imported clocks as well as models made in the United States. He also stocked European novelties. Advertisements during the beginning of the 1870s described Kroeber as an "importer and dealer in French, German and American clocks."

When a German immigrant sought employment in 1868, F. Kroeber accepted this man, Nicholas Mueller, as a partner. Mueller specialized in producing bronzed cast-metal figurines and inscribed-metal clock cases. This relationship only lasted about a year, however.

Kroeber began to create clock cases. He ordered movements from Connecticut makers. His clock business was successful, and he incorporated it as the F. Kroeber Clock Company. He was successful enough to open a second store in Manhattan's midtown area. In order to stock his store with interesting novelties, he traveled to Europe in the spring of 1888 to buy a variety of novelties—vases, candelabra, bronze figures, nickel and brass items, wood-cased pieces, and plush-covered novelties.

Kroeber created clock cases until 1899. Several, patented in 1869, looked like Victorian picture frames. Sometimes, however, he purchased metal cases from other companies.

He imported marble and china cases, but installed American movements in them. Kroeber also created a new finish, coating cast-iron clock cases so that they resembled porcelain. He called his patented product, "Porcelene." Soon Ansonia Clock Company produced clocks with the same porcelain-type finish and colors, so Kroeber sued Ansonia for infringing on his patent. In addition, Kroeber patented a pendulum that did not have to be taken off when a clock was moved.

Kroeber's 1888 catalog displayed more than 250 clocks, ninety percent of which were made in America. Business dropped after the Depression of 1893, though, so Kroeber was forced to close one store and move into smaller quarters. Unfortunately, he went bankrupt

F. Kroeber cast-iron black enameled mantel clock, gilded decorations, eight-day time & strike, ca. 1898, 12 1/2" h. $300.

in January 1904. After he lost his company, he worked for seven years as a clerk in a store watch and clock department. Kroeber died from tuberculosis on May 16, 1911.

Today, people who enjoy collecting unique clocks appreciate examples of his quality work. Collectors know his clocks bring higher prices and are more difficult to find than those made by some of the major clock companies.

Some authorities suspect, but have not proved, that Kroeber put his label on some mass-produced American and imported clocks. It is known that Kroeber had a label that read, "F. Kroeber, agent for New Haven, E. N. Welch, Jerome, Seth Thomas and other companies."

Collectors should carefully inspect clocks reputed to be made by Kroeber. A Kroeber label, dial, or marked Kroeber movement makes a clock desirable as well as costly, but it must be determined that there are no reproduction parts. A specialist in Kroeber clocks can be of great assistance.

As an aid in dating Kroeber clocks, the information that follows may answer questions relating to the age of a specific clock.

Kroeber Company Names and Addresses by Date

Name of Company	Address	Date
F. Kroeber	25 John St.	1865 – 1869
	10 Cortlandt St.	1869 – 1874
	8 Cortlandt St.	1874 – 1882
	14 Cortlandt St.	1883 – Feb. 1887
F. Kroeber Clock Company	14 Cortlandt St.	Feb. 1887 – Dec. 1887
	360 Broadway	Jan. 1888 – 1892
	360 Broadway & 14 Union Square*	1892 – March 1895
	360 Broadway	March 1895 – May 1899
F. Kroeber & Company	14 Maiden Lane	May 1899 – Feb. 1904
Mueller & Kroeber	25 John St. or 66 Beekman St.	1868 – 1869

*Clocks may not have been labeled with both addresses, so 360 Broadway may have been used from January 1888 through May 1899.

Lux and Keebler

Before establishing the Lux Clock Company in 1917, Paul Lux worked for the Waterbury Clock Company. His family, including his wife and two sons, Fred and Herman, worked together for several years trying to form a clock company that would make novelty clocks. Despite a fire that delayed their project and their sons marching off to fight in World War I, their perseverance and help from friends moved the project forward, inspired by their motto "Our Clocks Must Go–or We Go." When the two boys returned home from service, Lux clocks were ready to go to market.

Lux formed an association with the Keebler Company in Chicago. August C. Keebler, had Lux make clocks for him. A reciprocal agreement stated that each company could sell the same clocks, but they must be marketed with different names. Compressed molded wood was used to manufacture these clocks. One of their pendulette novelty clocks featured a black cat swinging its pendulum tail as its eyes moved. These clocks used a variety of themes such as Rudolf the Red Nose Reindeer, Woody Woodpecker, the Empire State Building, castles, bulldogs, clowns, , flowers, pirates, and other objects and animals. Clocks other than pendulettes featured current events, comic characters, patriotic themes, the Boy Scouts, and well known people ranging from Sally Rand (the fan dancer) to President Franklin D. Roosevelt. Many of these examples are shown in chapter 8: Novelty Clocks.

The variety of Lux novelty clocks is seemingly endless. These fun clocks cause people to smile. Owners of some models can smile too when they think of how their values have soared. The price of Lux wall clocks starts at $250 and climbs to a phenomenal $3,500 for the "Christmas Wreath."

Lux cuckoo pendulette, molded wood, bird sitting on the top, 30-hour, time only, spring driven, 4 x 6 1/2" h. **$55**.

Eli Terry

In 1792 to 1793, Eli Terry, Sr. showed that he was a man with creative ideas. He asked the question, "Why make one clock only?" It was easier to complete parts for several clocks at the same time, and Terry proceeded to do so. The floor clocks he made were originally called long-case or tall-case clocks. Now they are referred to as grandfather clocks. Shorter versions are called grandmother clocks.

From 1806 to 1809, Terry made four thousand

hang-up clock movements, dials, hands, and pendulums. He invented machines that helped with his work, including one that cut gear wheel teeth. He harnessed the waterpower available in Waterbury, Connecticut, to run his machines, and his employees, Silas Hoadley and Seth Thomas, assisted him. In 1810, Silas Hoadley and Seth Thomas bought Terry's plant. Terry moved to Plymouth Hollow, Connecticut, where he continued his work.

In approximately 1816, Terry patented a shelf clock that featured an outside escapement movement in a pillar-and-scroll case. Soon, around 1818 to 1824, the three men of the Terry family—Eli Sr., Eli Jr., and Henry—organized the firm Eli Terry and Sons of Plymouth, Connecticut. Their pillar-and-scroll clocks sold well. Each had a label that proclaimed: "Patent clock invented by Eli Terry made and sold at Plymouth, Connecticut by Eli Terry and Sons."

Terry clock labels varied, and their dates frequently overlapped. For example, from 1824 to 1827, Eli and brother Samuel were both listed on some labels; yet, from 1824 to 1830, other labels listed only Eli Terry Jr. Furthermore, from 1825 to 1830, some labels listed Eli Terry and son Henry,

Eli Terry pendulum candlestick novelty clock with china base on wooden frame, 6" d., 9" h., time only, original glass dome missing $300.

while from 1830 to 1841, other labels record the name Eli Terry Jr. and Company.

On December 22, 1831, Plymouth changed changed its name to Terrysville to honor Eli Terry Sr. In about 1834, Terry retired after a financially profitable career. To keep occupied, however, he made brass-movement clocks during his retirement years.

In the late 1840s, Silas Burnham Terry, Eli's youngest son, established the S. B. Terry Company to make clocks.

Eli Terry Sr. died in 1852 in the town that changed its name to honor him. His descendants did not forget their heritage. In 1852, Silas Burnham Terry and his son founded the Terry Clock Company in Winsted, Connec-ticut. The company remained in business until 1876. Interestingly, the spelling of the town name was changed slightly in 1872. By deleting the "s," Terrysville became Terryville.

The Willard Brothers

Four of the Willard brothers were clockmakers. Their names were Benjamin (1743-1803), the third child of twelve siblings; Simon (1753-1848), the eighth child; Ephram (life span not available), the ninth child; and Aaron (1757-1844), the tenth child. Very little has been written about Ephram and his activities. He apparently worked for a while in the area where his siblings worked, including Roxbury, Massachusetts. In 1798, he left the area. He was listed as a New York resident in 1805.

After completing his apprenticeship in 1764, Benjamin began making clocks in Grafton, Massachusetts. He soon moved to Boston and opened a shop on Roxbury Street where a colony of artists resided. There he made a variety of clock styles. In 1773 he ran an advertisement in the Boston Gazette that read, "Benjamin Willard at his shop in Roxbury Street ... has on sale musical clocks playing different tunes every day of the week and on Sunday a psalm tune." He further stated: "The music plays once every hour and does not obstruct the clock's motion in any way."

Simon was the second brother to enter the clockmaking trade. He became the most famous of the four siblings. Tall-case clocks (now called grandfathers) were the norm until Simon helped introduce shelf and wall clocks. Around 1800, he began working on an eight-day wall clock. It was patented on February 8, 1892, as his "Improved Timepiece." The pendulum was suspended from the front with the weight at the bottom that allowed the pendulum to be screwed down. This meant that the clock could be moved without damaging the suspension. Because of the clock's shape, it was called a banjo clock. The first models were time only. The clocks featured a clear seven-inch dial, fine hands, a mahogany case, and the glass was decorated with gold leaf. The weight-driven movement was so accurate that "it kept well within one minute's error a week." This beautiful instrument won acclaim at once and is still a popular style. Naturally, others desired to create similar clocks. They had to make slight changes, however, so as not to infringe on Simon's patent.

Simon also invented the lighthouse clock, which he patented in 1822. It had an octagonal base, a mahogany case, a tapered circular trunk, and a glass dome covering the eight-day alarm movement. An engraved brass dial with arrow hands completed the clock. The clock is on exhibit at the Metropolitan Museum of Art in New York City. His work is featured in other museums, too. For example, a ninety-two-inch-high Simon Willard grandfather clock with a white iron dial plus moon and calendar configuration is on display at the Henry Ford Museum in Greenfield Village, Dearborn, Michigan.

Simon advertised that he made church-steeple clocks as well as eight-day timepieces. But he was prolific as he was skilled; in a thirty-eight-year period, he made approximately four thousand clocks.

Simon's younger brother Aaron made banjo clocks, and with his brothers' help created thirty-hour wall timepieces. Soon, they and other makers fashioned the earliest known American shelf clocks. Their cases looked like the top section of tall-case clocks, earning the name, "Massachusetts half clocks."

The Willard Brothers contributed ideas that promoted and expanded the clock industry. Their clocks were durable and ran well because of their precise workmanship and use of hard brass.

Histories - Smaller Clock Manufacturers • Chapter 3 • 45

Other Small Clockmakers

Baird Advertiser

Ball Watch Company

E. M. Barnes

Birge & Mallory

Chauncey Boardman

W. Boardman

Brewster & Ingraham

J. C. Brown

J. C. Brown & Company

Burroughs Clock Company

L. F. & W. W. Carter

Chelsea Clock Company

Austin Chittenden

Forestville Manufacturing Company

Hopkins & Alfred Clock Co

L. Hubbell

C. & L. C. Ives

Chauncey Jerome

Jerome & Co.

Jerome Darrow & Company

Mark Leavenworth

Macomb Calendar Clock Company

Elisha Manross

March, Gilbert & Company

Mitchell, Atkins & Co.

Orton, Preston & Co.

George B. Owen Clock Company

Parker Clock Company

The Prentiss Clock Company

Roswell-Kimberly

Russell and Jones

Sidney Advertiser

Southern Calendar Clock Co.

Elmer Stennes

Eli Terry & Son

E. Terry & Sons

Eli Terry, Jr.

Samuel Terry

Terry Clock Company

Seth Thomas

M. Welton

William M. Wrigley Clock Company

Jerome & Co. rosewood transition shelf clock w/half columns, 30-hour time & strike, weight driven, ca. 1851, 15 x 25" h. **$250.**

Label from **Jerome & Co.** transition shelf clock. It reads, in part, "30-hour clocks, w/extra bushed movements, manufactured by Jerome & Co., New Haven, Conn. Instructions for setting the clock running & keeping it in order."

Chapter 4
Old Timers

In the 1700s, owning a clock was a status symbol. Each clock was handcrafted and was made only when an affluent person placed an order. The clockmaker frequently melted the brass in his own furnace, cast it, hammered it, turned it, and filed it. The dial, the hands, the works, the case—all the parts for the clock—were completed in one shop. Apprentices assisted as they learned the trade. As a result, the process was very expensive, and very few people could afford to buy a clock so painstakingly constructed.

The following eight artisans, applying their particular skills, were employed in making patent clocks:

1) the carpenter who made the cases,
2) the foundry man who formed the finials,
3) the artist who painted the glass tablet,
4) the goldsmith who made the gold leaf,
5) the diemaker who made the hands,
6) the craftsman who imported and applied the veneers to the cases, 7) the gluemakers who secured the dowels and blocks to keep the case together, and 8) the wood carver and the stencil artisan who added embellishments.

Banjo Clocks

A public or town clock was mentioned in town records as early as 1650. Citizens throughout the colonies believed strongly that every town needed a town clock.

Because handcrafted clocks required so many processes, a learner or apprentice needed the supervision of a master craftsman. A youth began his training at about fourteen years old and was bound by contract to a tradesman for seven years. The master taught the youth all aspects of the trade from the simple to the complex until he became proficient. He was paid no wages, but did receive room and board in his tutor's home. Because of the free labor provision, the clockmaker made more profit and often increased his business. At the completion of the contract, the master gave the apprentice a letter of recommendation. The following letter, dated July 13, 1796, is an example of such a recommendation:

This is to certify that Daniel Monroe, Jun. had served an apprenticeship of seven years with me the Subscriber, that he had been uncommonly faithful, honest, and industrious, and that I hereby acknowledge him capable of making any work that I manufacture and that I do pronounce him as one of the best workmen in America (signed) Simon Willard.

During the 1770s, brass founders did the initial preparation of the metal. By 1780, however, cast-brass parts could be purchased, and clockmakers did the finish work of turning, gear cutting, filing, and assembling. The industry was beginning to diversify,

Chelsea walnut banjo clock, time only w/single weight, made in Boston, ca. 1890, 39" h. **$3,500**.

Curtis reproduction rosewood banjo wall clock, time only, weight driven, 10 x 42" h. **$1,000**.

as different craftsmen became involved in the clockmaking process.

Extensive clockmaking was carried out in the colonies of Delaware, Maryland, Virginia, North Carolina, South Carolina, Georgia, Rhode Island, and New Hampshire. The study of the men involved and their clockmaking activities would provide the reader with a mini history of this colonial trade.

In the beginning of colonial clockmaking, handcrafting limited both the quantity of clocks manufactured and the ability to produce them inexpensively, but when machines that used waterpower were introduced, production greatly increased.

By the middle of the eighteenth century, Philadelphia was a center for the manufacture of clock cases and movements, and the repair of clocks and watches. Philadelphia's principal products were tall clocks and some bracket clocks. The bracket clock has erroneously been called a mantel clock. Although the clocks are similar, the bracket clock is designed to rest on a bracket affixed to a wall, rather than rest on a mantel or shelf. Also, bracket clocks pre-dated mantel clocks by about fifty years.

Philadelphia's tall clocks and bracket clocks were not made by mass production. The clock makers, as artisans, followed their tradition of handcrafting their products, but this method of clockmaking decreased to such an extent that by 1850 few clocks

Wm. L. Gilbert eight-day banjo clock, time & "bim-bam" strike on two steel rods, ca. 1929, 29 1/2" h. **$275.**

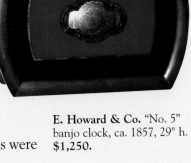

E. Howard & Co. "No. 5" banjo clock, ca. 1857, 29" h. **$1,250.**

in the Philadelphia area were handcrafted any longer. The craftsmen's inability to compete with the Connecticut clockmakers, who produced inexpensive clocks, caused their eventual demise.

Perhaps the most noted clockmaker from the Philadelphia school was David Rittenhouse, a mathematician, surveyor, astronomer, and clockmaker. His most outstanding creation was a nine-foot masterpiece that could play ten musical tunes on fifteen bells. This clock, made in 1774, originally sold for $640 and is on display at the Drexel Institute in Philadelphia.

The Shakers, who established themselves in upstate New York after the Revolutionary War, engaged in some clockmaking. Their creations were usually without ornate decorations or striking mechanisms. The earliest Shaker clockmaker was Amos Jewett (1753-1834), who made tall clocks with printed paper dials. He numbered his clocks so they could easily be identified. For example, number twelve was made in 1789 and number thirty-eight was made seven years later.

The Boston area is known for the Willard family, who became prominent clockmakers. Two of the sons, Benjamin and Ephraim, mainly produced tall clocks, while Simon and Aaron made shelf clocks as well as tall clocks. Some clocks attributed to the brothers include a miniature shelf clock (circa 1780) and a kidney dial shelf clock (circa 1795) by Aaron, and a patent alarm lighthouse clock (circa 1833) by Simon.

Ingraham Clock Co. "Nyanza" banjo clock, ca. 1915, 18 1/2" h. **$140.**

Little & Eastman eight-day weight-driven banjo clock, ca. 1907, 33" h. **$1,000.**

Simon Willard was proud of his newly invented "Alarum Timepiece" and touted it in an advertisement that read, "...will run 8 days with one winding, and keep exact time; there is an alarum affixed to them, which, when set, will not fail to go off at the hour you wish to rise. The case is about 16 inches high, and easily moved to any part of the house without putting it out of order. The whole of the clock works is enclosed with a handsome glass, and is wound up without taking it off, which prevents the dirt from getting into it."

Wooden movements, which were easier to make and less costly than hand-fashioned brass movements, came into use around 1800. Cases for clocks were most often made of mahogany, although it was more expensive than the wood that was available locally. When local wood was used, the species varied according to its abundance geographically. In Pennsylvania, for example, cases were sometimes made of walnut and maple, whereas in New England, pine and cherry were the primary woods used.

Clock works operated by falling weights required large cases to provide an adequate dropping height. Consequently, early weight-driven shelf clocks were tall.

Clocks with heavy weights were expensive to ship. Because of this, empty "tin cans" (sheet-iron cans), rather than heavy weights, were shipped with the clocks. The recipient could fill these containers

Massachusetts rope front banjo, ca. 1850, 34" h. **$1,025**.

New Haven "Waring" eight-day time & strike banjo clock, ca. 1923, 40" h. **$110**.

New Haven "Waring" eight-day spring-driven banjo clock, strikes hours on steel rod, ca. 1827, 39" h. **$230.**

with sand or stones to provide the weight necessary to operate the clock properly.

In the late 1700s, paper dials could be purchased in books of 24, 48, or 96. They were pasted on wooden panels or iron plates to form clock faces.

Three unique shelf clocks are the cottage, beehive, and acorn. The acorn clock design—both shelf and wall style—originated in America. The Forestville Manufacturing Company made all three models, installing eight-day fusee movements in them. Jonathan Clarke Brown was the manager of the Forestville factory during the mid 1800s.

The cottage clock, first made around 1875, is a smaller form of the Connecticut shelf clock. Most examples have thirty-hour movements and wooden cases that are normally less than one foot in height, with either flat or three-sided tops. Most were made in the last quarter of the nineteenth century.

Simon Willard patented the banjo wall clock in 1802. He called it his "Improved Timepiece" but it was dubbed "banjo" because it resembled that instrument in shape. The "banjo" was a native American type and not a copy of a previously produced European clock. Originally it was time only and reputedly cost $35.

The girandole clock, credited to Lemuel Curtis, is similar in design to the banjo clock but larger, with a circular rather than a rectangular base frame. Carved acanthus leaves add a decorative touch, and an ornately carved American eagle was frequently poised at the top of the clock.

New Haven "Waring" banjo clock, ca. 1928, 39" h. **$200.**

Produced between 1814 and 1829, many consider it the most beautiful clock case ever created in America.

Among the pictured banjo wall clocks found in this book are several expensive and hard-to-find examples by E. Howard & Company. Another rare banjo wall clock, with Westminster chimes, is the Ansonia "Girandole."

The E. Howard Clock Company, led by Edward Howard (1813-1904), who had served as an apprentice to Aaron Willard at 16, produced a series of banjo regulators as seen in an 1858 company catalog. He eventually became a prominent maker of clocks, including wall and tower clocks, banjos, regulators, grandfathers, and figure-eights. Tower clocks were built into towers or steeples of public buildings for the public's use. Several of these models have been reproduced. Howard's clocks rank higher in value than most of the other manufactured clocks of like kind.

The long-case clock, commonly called a grandfather clock, was first made in England in the latter part of the seventeenth century, shortly after the Restoration of 1660. Similar clocks were also appearing in Europe around this time. These clocks were approximately seven feet high, featuring brass dials, until painted dials appeared around 1770.

New Haven "Welton" eight-day banjo clock, ca. 1928, 25 1/4" h. **$110.**

New Haven "Winetka" eight-day time & strike banjo clock, mahogany case, ca. 1928, 18" h. **$410.**

Until mahogany was introduced, long-case clock cases were commonly made of walnut with marquetry designs. Satinwood and rosewood were two other woods used. Oak was used, as well, but only for cheaper clocks. The cases hid the pendulum and weights and kept the works dust free. Often the cases were highly polished and adorned with rich ornamental touches. The dials were richly decorated and the mechanisms contained bells of various sizes, which struck on the hours and quarter hours. Later, the clocks registered the day of the week, the date, and the month. At the end of the seventeenth century, a good London-made grandfather clock with a highly polished walnut and ebony case cost about $60.

Called hall clocks, floor clocks, tall-case clocks, or long-case clocks, these clocks were the first to be assembled in the colonies. Made throughout the colonies, they were modifications of the English styles. Clockmakers, in general, copied the styles and patterns used in their homeland.

All of the colonies made long-case clocks, but Pennsylvania and Massachusetts produced the greatest number. These early clocks had either a brass or wooden movement and operated for one day or eight days.

A Simon Willard grandfather clock is on display at the Henry Ford Museum in Greenfield Village,

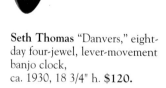

Seth Thomas "Danvers," eight-day four-jewel, lever-movement banjo clock, ca. 1930, 18 3/4" h. **$120.**

New Haven walnut banjo wall clock, beveled glass w/New Haven on dial, time only, ca. 1895, 25" h. **$200.**

Dearborn, Michigan. The Ford museum also has on exhibit a typical Thomas Harland clock made around 1780. He was a renowned clockmaker and the first to use interchangeable parts and mass production principles from 1791 onward. Another of Harland's grandfather clocks is on display at the Metropolitan Museum of Art in New York City.

A David Rittenhouse tall-case clock is on display at the Henry Francis du Pont Winterthur Museum, in Winterthur, Delaware. The clock, made in 1755, has a brass movement and a tulip poplar case.

The Waltham Clock Company's reproductions of Willard banjo clocks were listed in its 1928 catalog. The cases were solid mahogany or walnut with gilt or crackle finishes. Each could be ordered with a brass eagle or carved acorn ornament on top. The glass panels were available in a variety of designs: Washington/Mt. Vernon; Lone Ship; English Castle; Boston State House; Monticello/Jefferson; Perry's Victory; Wayside Inn; Independence Hall/Liberty Bell; Constitution and Guerriere; and Old Ironsides.

Thomas Harland of Norwich, Connecticut, who came to the American colonies from London in 1773, was among the clockmakers who plied their trade before the advent of mass production. He worked for approximately thirty-five years, had many apprentices, and probably produced more tall clocks than any other Connecticut tradesman. He may have produced an average of 25 clocks per year. Among his talents were making and repairing watches and making musical and spring-driven timepieces. Attributed to

Seth Thomas "Ramsgate" eight-day, seven-jewel, lever-movement banjo wall clock, ca. 1929, 21" h. **$225.**

Seth Thomas mahogany banjo clock, eight-day time only, ca. 1938, 6 1/2 x 24" h. **$100.**

Harland is a musical bracket clock made in 1780 that was the envy of local tradesmen. One of his clocks played six tunes. Upon his death in 1807, he left an estate of $3,500 in tinware, clocks, watches, jewelry, and tradesman's tools.

The American Empire Period, spanning 1825 to 1840, followed the Federal period and preceded the Victorian. Representative models of this period include the looking-glass clock and the triple-decker clock. These eight-day mahogany-veneered clocks were principally manufactured by the Forestville Manufacturing Company around 1840.

"Old-timer" clocks can be catergorized as pillar-and-scroll, looking glass, transition, and OG. They were made by manufacturers such as E. Terry & Sons; Mark Leavenworth; Eli Terry; Samuel Terry; Eli Terry & Son; Mitchell, Atkins & Company; Austin Chittenden; Marsh, Gilbert & Company; Jerome, Darrow & Company; Eli Terry Jr.; and Seth Thomas.

Eli Terry patented the pillar-and-scroll clock, probably America's first mass-produced clock, in 1816. It evolved from his plain box case and had thirty-hour wooden works. Other makers varied the case somewhat so they could copy the idea without infringing on Terry's patent.

Eli Terry (1772-1852) has earned the reputation as "The Father of the Clock Making Industry." His clockmaking career started in 1793 and spanned sixty years. He introduced ways that changed American clockmaking from handcrafting to man-

Seth Thomas mahogany stained banjo clock, time only. Pictures of George Washington & Mount Vernon on the tablets & the eagle on the top make this a uniquely American clock, ca. 1936, 6 1/2 x 24" h. **$275.**

Seth Thomas miniature banjo clock w/eight-day back-wind lever movement, ca. 1920, 19 3/4" h. **$170.**

ufacturing. The clocks he made include wooden tall clocks, wooden shelf clocks, and a variety of brass clocks. His name is still known and respected in the clockmaking industry today. Eli Terry's development of the wooden shelf clock contributed to the growth of his business because the old-fashioned tall clocks were losing popularity. One reason for this was that they were difficult to transport. A shelf clock, however, being considerably smaller, was easily transported and could be readily moved from room to room in family homes.

Between 1820 and 1840, Connecticut clockmakers were busy making wooden shelf clocks. Brass shelf clocks were a thing of the future. Brass clocks were more costly to make than wooden varieties, in some cases, three times more expensive. Many clock companies, however, developed an interest in the cheap brass-movement clock. Prior to the American Civil War, spring-driven clocks came into vogue. After the American Civil War, expensive brass springs were replaced by steel springs. Shelf clocks with wooden works usually contain thirty-hour movements. Eight-day examples are unusual.

One of Terry's competitors was Joseph Ives, who began making brass clocks in 1818. Chauncey Boardman (1789-1857) also became interested in producing shelf clocks.

The looking-glass clock had a mirror tablet

Elmer Stennes signed weight-driven banjo clock, ca. 1972, 40" h. **$3,000.**

Elmer Stennes mahogany ribbon stripe banjo clock, marked MCIP (made clock in prison), one weight, time only, 7" dial, 44" h. **$2,900.**

instead of the usual picture or design. Thrifty housewives liked the combination clock-mirror. Chauncey Jerome claimed it as his invention even though his "bronze looking-glass clock" with its bronze-colored pilasters that gave it its name, was patented about three years after Joseph Ives patented a looking-glass clock in 1822.

"Transition" was the name given to certain clocks in the late 1820s, most of which had thirty-hour weight-driven movements. They were carved or stenciled and frequently had paw-type feet. Often they featured side columns and included a stenciled or carved top slat. They were an in-between style, appearing about the time the pillar-and-scroll was at the height of its popularity and the OG was new.

The OG (ogee) clock was a continuous favorite from about 1825 until 1920. Its box frame featured an ogee, or S-curved, veneered (usually mahogany) door molding and front. The OG had a decorated tablet. Early one-day weight-driven examples were approximately twenty-six inches high to accommodate their falling weights, whereas eight-day types usually measured about thirty-four inches high. Later, fifteen- or sixteen-inch-high spring-driven, thirty-hour miniature OG clocks became available.

Waltham "No. 1550" eight-day miniature banjo clock using Waltham's sturdy jeweled movement w/stem wind, ca. 1928, 21" h. **$1,050.**

Waltham Willard-model weight-driven banjo clock w/cross-banded case, ca. 1930, 42" h. **$1,900.**

During this time, the following companies represented the wide range of OG clock manufacturers who were reaping profits through the sale of this popular clock:

Waltham Willard-model banjo clock in mahogany case, ca. 1935, 40 1/2" h. **$1,300.**

Manufacturer	Location
Ansonia Clock Company	Ansonia
Boardmen and Wells	Bristol
Brewster and Ingrahams	Bristol
Forestville Mfg. Company	Bristol
C. (Chauncey) Jerome	Bristol
Jerome and Company	New Haven
Manross, Pritchard and Company	Bristol
Seth Thomas	Plymouth
Seth Thomas	Thomaston
Smith and Goodrich	Bristol
Smith and Brothers	New York City
Henry Terry	Plymouth
Terry and Andrews	Bristol
Waterbury Clock Company	Waterbury
E. N. Welch Manufacturing Company	Bristol
Riley Whiting	Winchester

The following shows the exact words found on the backboard label of a Seth Thomas time-and-strike shelf clock with an alarm.

Waltham Willard-model banjo clock w/dial signed both "Waltham" & "Smith Patterson Co.," ca. 1925, 40" h. **$1,325.**

Thirty-Hour Spring Clocks
Seth Thomas
Thomaston, Conn.
Warranted Good

Directions for setting the clock running. Place the clock in a perpen-dicular position. Oil the pattetes or ends of the part commonly called the VERGE; the pin on which the verge plays, and the wire, which carries the pendulum, at the place where it touches the rod. One drop is sufficient for the whole. Hang on the pendulum ball, then put on key with handle down, and turn toward the figure VI and turn steadily until the clock is wound.

If the Clock should go too fast, lower the ball by means of a screw at the bottom of the pendulum; if too slow raise it.

If the hands want moving, do it by means of the longest, turning it at any time forward, but never backward, when the Clock is within fifteen minutes of striking; and in no case further than to carry the minute hand to the figure XII.

Should the Clock by any means strike wrong, it may be made to strike right by raising the small wire hanging near the bell.

Waltham eight-day lever-movement banjo clock, ca. 1930, 42" h. **$1,000.**

Waltham three-quarter-size lever-movement banjo wall clock, ca. 1920, 30" h. **$500.**

Waltham mahogany banjo wall clock, in the Willard style, ivory enamel dial, Perry's Victory on glass tablet, weight driven, ca. 1929, 10 1/2 x 41" h. **$2,500.**

Grandfather Clocks

Colonial Mfg. "Model 1216," five-tube grandfather clock, ca. 1919, 87" h. **$1,350.**

American eight-day grandfather clock, w/mahogany case, brass works, tin can weights, & painted dial, ca. 1820, 90" h. **$7,500.**

Herschede Hall Clock Co. "Model 515," mahogany case grandfather clock, w/five tubes, Westminster chime, rolling moon, & trademark Herschede crown in the arch, ca. 1962, 75 1/2" h. **$1,550.**

Herschede Hall Clock Co. "Model 215," mahogany case grandfather clock, w/nine-tubes, Whittington & Westminster tunes, rolling moon, ca. 1950, 80" h. **$2,200.**

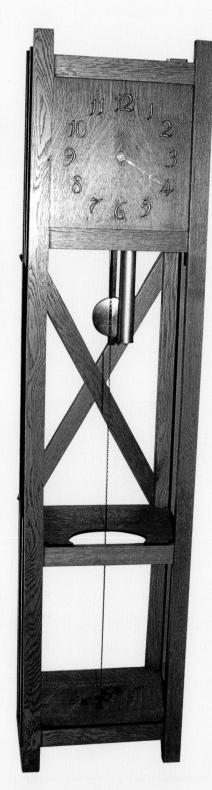

Silas Hoadley scarce eight-day pull-wind grandfather clock w/tin canister weights & cast-iron pendulum bob, striking wheels in front of front plate & escapement outside back plate, ca. 1820, 90" h. to top of finial. **$1,400.**

Monitor Clock Works (Medina, New York), mission-oak floor clock w/works, 16 1/2 x 68" h. **$795.**

New Hampshire grandfather clock, cherry case, eight-day wood plate movement w/brass & steel gears, unsigned, but attributed to Abijah Gould of Hollis, New Hampshire, ca. 1810, 83" h. **$1,850.**

Seth Thomas mahogany custom made "grandfather look" floor clock, w/OG upper section sitting on top of lower storage section, 30-hour, 19 x 77 1/2" h. **$700.**

View of **Seth Thomas** "grandfather look" clock w/bottom door closed.

Waltham mahogany grandfather clock, made from a kit, brass weights & pendulum, beveled glass, applied brass decorations, moon dial, early 1900s, 91" h. **$1,750.**

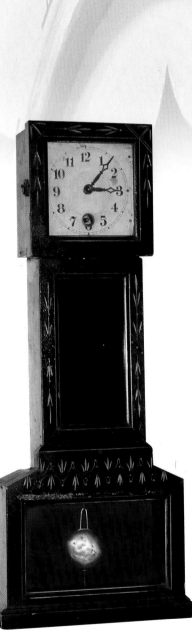

Luman Watson 30-hour wooden movement grandfather clock, w/cherry case & mahogany accents, ca. 1820, 94" h. **$4,200.**

Yale Clock Co. "Grandfather" 30-hour timepiece, ca. 1880, 16" h. **$300.**

OG Clocks

J. C. Brown mahogany shelf clock, eight-day time & strike, 16 1/2 x 29" h. **$350.**

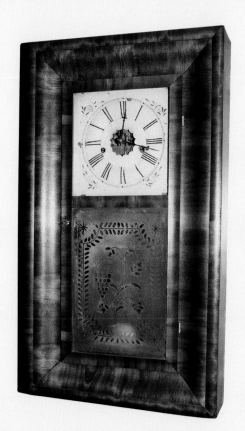

J. C. Brown rosewood double OG, original tablet, eight-day time & strike, ca. 1855, 16 1/2 x 29" h. **$400.**

J. C. Brown rosewood oversized OG, eight-day time, strike, & alarm, ca. 1855, 16 1/2 x 31" h. **$350.**

J. C. Brown rosewood wall hanging OG, 30-hour, time & strike, reverse painting on tablet, 15 1/2 x 25 1/2" h. **$350.**

Forestville mahogany OG, w/maker J. C. Brown on the label, eight-day time & strike, weight driven, ca. 1855, 16 x 29" h. **$400.**

Forestville mahogany OG, made by J. C. Brown, eight-day time & strike, weight driven, ca. 1848, 17 x 29" h. **$550.**

Chauncey Jerome mahogany miniature round band OG, eight-day time, strike, & alarm, tablet not original, ca. 1868, 11 x 16 1/2" h. **$350.**

Chauncey Jerome invented the case & movement of OG clocks. Shown here is one of his mahogany OG clocks w/brass dial, 30-hour, time & strike, ca. 1845, 15 1/2 x 26" h. **$300.**

Chauncey Jerome rosewood veneer OG mirror wall clock, 30-hour, time & strike, ca. 1848, 15 x 25 1/2" h. **$250.**

Label from a **Chauncey Jerome** OG shelf clock. It reads, in part, "Patent brass clocks, manufactured and sold by Chauncey Jerome, New Haven, Conn. Warranted good. Directions for setting the clock running and keeping it in order…"

Chauncey Jerome mahogany OG, replaced picture on tablet, ca. 1845, 15 1/2 x 26" h. **$300.**

Chauncey Jerome walnut veneer OG shelf clock, 30-hour, weight driven, ca. 1885, 26" h. **$350.**

William S. Johnson rosewood miniature double OG shelf clock, 30-hour, ca. 1860, 12 x 18 1/2" h. **$225.**

Label from **Elisha Manross** OG shelf clock. It reads, "30-hour clocks, warranted good. Made and sold by Elisha Manross, Bristol, Conn."

Elisha Manross mahogany double OG, 30-hour, time & strike, ca. 1845, 15 1/2 x 26" h. **$300.**

Elisha Manross mahogany OG shelf clock, 30-hour, time & strike, ca. 1848, 15 1/2 x 43" h. **$300.**

Manross Prichard & Co. mahogany OG shelf clock, ca. 1850, 16 x 26 1/2" h. **$350.**

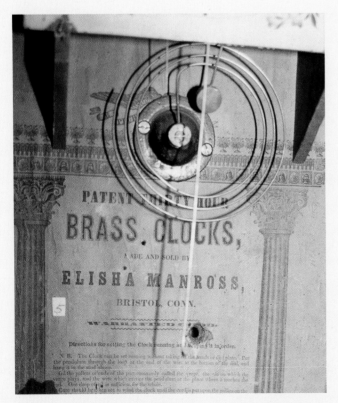

Label from **Elisha Manross** OG shelf clock. It reads, in part, "Patent thirty hour brass clocks, made and sold by Elisha Manross, Bristol, Conn. Warranted good. Directions for setting the clock running and keeping it in order."

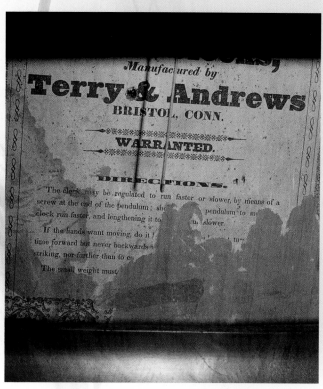

Label of **Terry & Andrews** OG shelf clock. It reads in part: "Manufactured by Terry & Andrews, Bristol, Conn. Warranted."

Terry & Andrews mahogany OG shelf clock, 30-hour, time & strike w/wooden dial. Terry & Andrews were in business two years & helped found the Ansonia Clock Company, ca. 1848, 15 x 26" h. **$300.**

Seth Thomas mahogany OG shelf clock w/weights, 30-hour time & strike. **$160.**

Seth Thomas mahogany round-band OG shelf clock, 30-hour, pre-1864, 11 x 16 1/2" h. **$125.**

Seth Thomas mahogany miniature mirror round band OG, 30-hour, time, strike, & alarm, 11 x 16 1/2" h. **$185.**

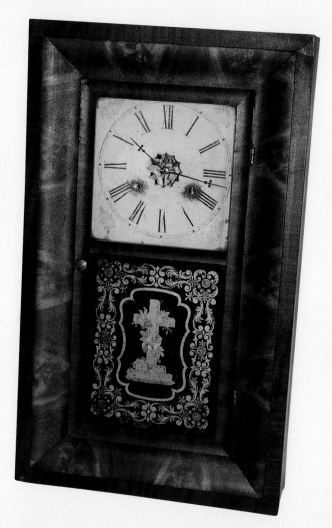

Seth Thomas rosewood OG made in Plymouth Hollow, eight-day time & strike, weight driven, ca. 1860, 15 1/2 x 25 1/2" h. **$250.**

Seth Thomas rosewood miniature, round band OG, 30-hour time & strike, ca. 1880, 10 1/2 x 16 1/2" h. **$250.**

Seth Thomas rosewood double OG, eight-day time & strike, weight driven, 15 x 25 1/2" h. **$450.**

Seth Thomas rosewood round band OG, eight-day time & strike, weight driven, ca. 1885, 15 x 25" h. **$450.**

Label from **Seth Thomas** OG shelf clock. It reads, "Eight Day Weight Clocks, Seth Thomas, Thomaston, Conn., Warranted Good."

E. N. Welch rosewood OG, 30-hour, time & strike, ca. 1875, 15 x 26" h. $300.

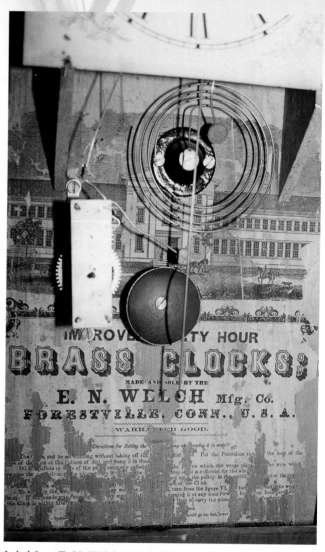

Label from E. N. Welch OG shelf clock. It reads, "Improved 30-Hour Brass Clocks Made and Sold By E. N. Welch Mfg. Co., Forestville, Conn., Warranted Good."

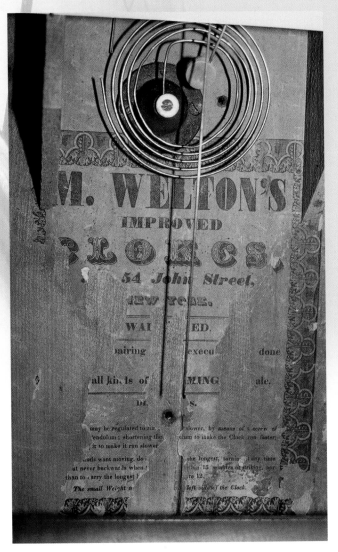

M. Welton label on OG shelf clock. It reads, in part, "M. Welton's improved clokes, 54 John Street, New York. Warranted." Note the misspelling of clocks on the label.

M. Welton mahogany, mirror door OG shelf clock, w/repainted dial. Welton made both clocks & cases, 30-hour, time & strike, ca. 1845, 16 x 26" h. **$300.**

Shelf Clocks

Birge, Peck & Co., triple-decker shelf clock w/eight-day time & strike strap brass movement, ca. 1855, 36 1/2" h. **$2,400.**

Birge, Mallory & Company triple-decker shelf clock, brass strap movement invented by Joseph Ives, painted wood dial, original bottom glass tablet, eight-day weight driven, ca. 1845, 17 x 38" h. **$700.**

Boardman and Wells, half-column & splat shelf clock, w/30-hour alarm wood movement & alarm, ca. 1840, 31 1/2" h. **$150.**

Forestville Manufacturing Company eight-day movement, mirror shelf clock, ca. 1845, 36" h. **$360.**

Forestville Manufacturing Company, also called J. C. Brown, mahogany transition wall clock w/gilded columns, eight-day time & strike, weight driven, 18 x 35" h. **$500.**

Forestville Manufacturing Company half-column & splat shelf clock w/30-hour wood movement, ca. 1835, 33 1/4" h. **$300.**

E. O. Goodwin rosewood shelf clock, w/gold leaf stenciling on case, eight-day time & strike, ca. 1850s, 9 1/2 x 15" h. **$800.**

Asaph Hall flat-column & splat shelf clock w/30-hour wood movement, ca. 1832, 34 1/2" h. **$600.**

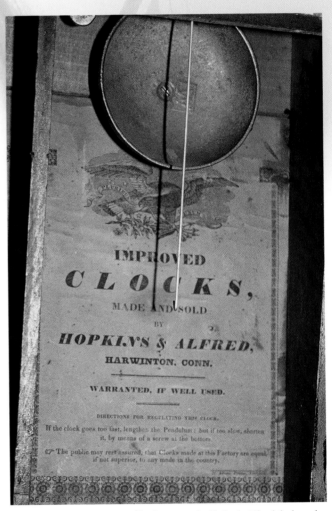

Label from **Hopkins & Alfred** mirror shelf clock. The label reads, "Improved clocks, made & sold by Hopkins & Alfred Clock Co., Harwinton, Conn. Warranted if well used."

Hopkins & Alfred Clock Co. mahogany mirror shelf clock, wooden works, weight driven, time & strike, ca. 1825, 17 x 30 1/2" h. **$500.**

Elisha Hotchkiss mahogany mirror shelf clock, 30-hour, time & strike, weight driven w/wooden dial & movement, top repainted but all original. Mirror clocks were very popular during the first half of the 19th c., dated 1835, **$400.**

C. & L. C. Ives triple-decker mahogany, shelf clock w/side pillars & ball feet, ca. 1835, 18 x 38" h. **$700.**

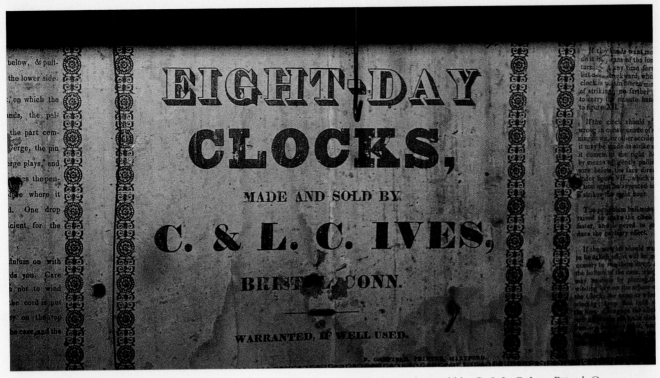

Label from **C. & L. C. Ives** triple-decker shelf clock. It reads, "Eight-day clocks, made & sold by C. & L. C. Ives, Bristol, Conn. Warranted if well used."

Wooden dial to **C. & L. C. Ives** triple-decker shelf clock. Notice the opening above the center which allows one to see the movement.

Brass strap movement from **C. & L. C. Ives** triple-decker shelf clock.

Jeromes & Darrow half-column & splat shelf clock w/30-hour wood movement, ca. 1830, 33 1/2" h. **$325.**

George Mitchell half-column & splat shelf clock w/30-hour wood movement, ca. 1831, 35 1/2" h. **$250.**

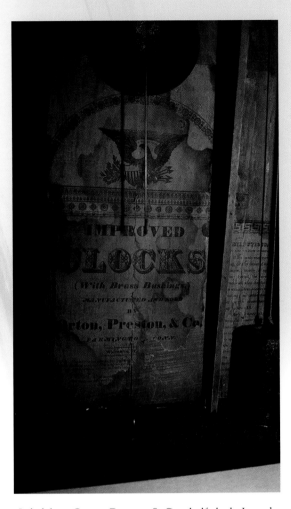

Label from **Orton, Preston & Co.** shelf clock. It reads, "Improved clocks (w/brass bushings) manufactured and sold by Orton, Preston & Co., Farmington, Conn."

Orton, Preston & Co. mahogany shelf clock, w/side columns, wooden movement, 30-hour, single weight, ca. 1828-1835, 16 1/2 x 31 1/2" h. **$395.**

Daniel Pratt, Jr. cornice-top shelf clock, w/30-hour time & strike & iron backplate, ca. 1842, 21 1/2" h. **$225.**

Seth Thomas rosewood pillar wall clock, original tablets, gilt columns, eight-day weight driven, prior to 1863 (Plymouth Hollow), 16 1/2" w., 32" h. **$550.**

Seth Thomas mahogany Empire-style shelf clock w/visible pendulum, eight-day time & strike w/alarm feature, 10 1/2 x 16" h. **$270.**

Unknown maker, mahogany shelf clock, side columns, time & strike, weight driven, label in clock names Covington, Indiana, & lists the makers as "Arwood & Cor—" **$250.**

Seth Thomas (Plymouth Hollow) rosewood wall clock, 1850-1863, with cornice and columns, original tablets with reverse painting, eight-day, time and strike, weight-driven, 16 1/2 x 32" h. $600.

Waterbury mahogany weight clock, has lantern pinions vs. cut teeth, bottom tablet is a replacement, ca. 1840s, 15 1/2 x 26" h. **$150.**

Unknown maker, mahogany-case shelf clock w/30-hour time, strike, & alarm brass movement, ca. 1850, 28 1/2" h. **$110.**

Inside label of a **Waterbury** mahogany Empire-style 1830s clock, eight-day time & strike, 16 x 24" h. **$295.**

Chapter 5
Wall Clocks

Many of the earliest wall clocks for use in schools, offices, and churches originated in Connecticut. Octagon clocks, among the most common, were frequently called "schoolhouse clocks." They were also popular in large workplaces or factories to keep employees informed of the time. The large round-dial timepieces known as gallery clocks could easily be read because of their size. Gallery clocks, usually manufactured in eight-day models, have been available since 1845.

An extremely useful wall clock was the regulator because its accuracy enabled it to be used to as a standard for other timekeepers. For example, it was used in jewelry store windows, where passersby could check to see if their watches were running correctly. Railroad stations also used regulators to make sure trains ran on schedule. As time passed, however, a great number of clocks called regulators, or those with this name on their tablets, were not accurate enough to be so named. "Regulator" had just become a generic term for a hanging wall clock.

Advertising Clocks

Two companies, Edward P. Baird of Plattsburgh, New York, and The Sidney Advertiser Company of Sidney, New York, were active in the manufacture of advertising clocks. From about 1895 to 1900, Baird made wooden advertising clocks with embossed or painted ads encircling the dials. The Sidney company used sound devices in its clocks. For instance, one clock had a bell that rang and advertising drums that turned every five minutes.

"Wag-on-the-wall" clocks produced by Waterbury were a series of oak hanging clocks, either weight or spring driven. Waterbury called these "study clocks" and used numbers to identify them. "Wag-on-the-wall" clocks were sold without a case and were the earliest wall clock made. Gideon Roberts (1749-1813) made an all-wooden "wag-on-the-wall" in the late 1700s. Metal plates enclosed the movement but the exposed pendulum swung below the clock's body.

In an early 1900 catalog, the Ansonia Clock Company featured wall regulators named after the following female regents: Queen Anne, Queen Charlotte, Queen Elizabeth, Queen Isabelle, Queen Jane, Queen Mab, Queen Mary, and Queen Victoria. The clocks were eight-day strikers with eight-inch dials. They

American Insurance Company (Newark, N. J.) advertising wall clock, 7 x 9 1/2" h. **$225**.

Baird advertising wall clock, eight-day time only, spring driven, ca. 1896, 31" h. **$1,500**.

averaged between thirty-seven and forty-two inches high and cost less than $20. The cases were available in black walnut, mahogany, or oak. All the clocks except the Queen Mary were available in the popular oak.

Wall clocks were occasionally made in Mission-style, which featured a plain, simple design of straight lines in sturdy oak. They remained in fashion from 1900 until the late 1920s. The 1960s showed a rebirth of mission furniture and reproductions in that style.

Although calendar clocks did not appear until the mid-1800s, a calendar movement was put in a tall case clock in England in 1660. Almost two hundred years later, in 1853, J. H. Hawes of Ithaca, New York, was the first known American to patent a simple calendar clock mechanism. The Ithaca Calendar Clock Company, formed in 1865, used Henry B. Horton's perpetual roller-type calendar-clock patent.

Bulova electric wall clock, 16 x 16" h. **$110**.

Coca-Cola electric wall clock, 16 x 16" h. **$110**.

The difference between a perpetual calendar clock and a simple calendar clock lies in the manner in which they account for the days in a year. The perpetual clock indicates the day of the week, the month, and the date. It is self-adjusting to allow for leap year. The simple calendar clock, on the other hand, requires an occasional manual adjustment to make it accurate.

Waterbury perpetual-calendar clocks could be furnished with languages other than English. Spanish, Portuguese, French, German, Swedish, and Italian calendar clocks became available in 1881.

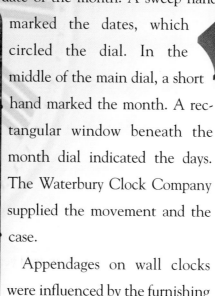

One of the clockmakers who developed a calendar dial was Charles W. Feishtinger. The dial showed the day of the week, the month, and the date of the month. A sweep hand marked the dates, which circled the dial. In the middle of the main dial, a short hand marked the month. A rectangular window beneath the month dial indicated the days. The Waterbury Clock Company supplied the movement and the case.

Appendages on wall clocks were influenced by the furnishing style of the Victorian Era, named after England's Queen Victoria, who reigned from 1837 to 1901. In the later half of the 1800s, both drop and upright carved finals, curved moldings and carvings, including heads, were used on clocks as well as furniture. Incised carving prevailed around 1870. Although oak and mahogany were occasionally used for clock cases, walnut was the clockmaker's choice.

The pendulum is one element that wall clocks have in common. The pendulum is a weight, often ornamental, that swings from a fixed point in a regular beat so it can regulates a clock's movement. Galileo (1564-1642) first conceived of using a pendulum to regulate a clock after observing a swinging lamp. In 1657, Christaan Huygens

Ever-Ready eight-day wall clock, by American Safety Razor Corporation, 12 1/2 x 18" h. **$2,495**.

W. L. Gilbert dark stained wall clock advertising Sauer's Extracts; glass etched & coins are gold leafed, eight-day time only, spring driven, 40" h. **$2,750**.

actually built a working clock using a pendulum.

The weight at the end of the pendulum rod is often ornamental, as well as necessary. It may be round or geometrical in shape and can be fitted with decorative appendages; examples include either a man's head or a woman's head in low relief. Crystal, Sandwich glass, and wooden examples are common. Although French clocks used genuine mercury pendulum bobs, American models used imitation mercury.

Brooks Palmer, in his work, *The Book of American Clocks*, reminds readers that the term "bob" is commonly used incorrectly. He points out that "a pendulum has three parts—the pendulum rod and the pendulum ball, which most people call the bob, and the real bob, which is the wire loop threaded for the regulating nut."

Lowering the bob on a pendulum rod lengthens its swing so the clock goes slower, while raising the bob shortens the swing so the clock goes faster. The rule can be difficult to remember. Fortunately, the four-word rhyme, "lower, slower; higher, sprier" makes it much easier to recall.

E. Ingraham wall clock advertising Ever-Ready Safety Razor, time only, 18" d., 29" h. **$4,000**.

Sessions oak regulator wall clock w/advertisement, "Chew Stronghold Plug," on lower tablet w/star & arch molding, time only, late 1800s, 16 1/2 x 38" h. **$875**.

Sessions oak regulator wall clock w/advertisement, "Drink Mission Orange Drink" on lower tablet, second Mission advertisement is above clock, eight-day time only, early 1900s, 17 x 37" h. **$925.**

Seth Thomas "Regulator No. 2," w/advertising that reads, Greenleaf & Crosby Co, Jewelers, 25 E. Bay St., Jacksonville, also at St. Augustine & Palm Beach, ca. 1890, 35" h. **$900**

Waterbury advertising wall clock w/"Nesler Bros., Dubuque, Iowa" on lower tablet, eight-day time only, 12 1/2 x 20" h. **$2,500.**

Waterbury oak store regulator w/Coca-Cola advertisement on bottom tablet, time & strike (most of these are time only), top tablet is original but bottom is replaced, 16 x 36" h. **$500.**

Waterbury oak jeweler's regulator wall clock advertising Odell Jewelry Store, Quincy, Illinois, time only, 37" h. **$700.**

Calendar Clocks

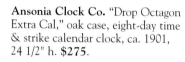

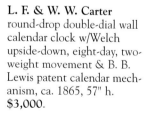

Ansonia Clock Co. "Drop Octagon Extra Cal," oak case, eight-day time & strike calendar clock, ca. 1901, 24 1/2" h. **$275**.

L. F. & W. W. Carter round-drop double-dial wall calendar clock w/Welch upside-down, eight-day, two-weight movement & B. B. Lewis patent calendar mechanism, ca. 1865, 57" h. **$3,000**.

L. F. & W. W. Carter eight-day, weight-driven, double-dial calendar wall clock w/Welch movement & B. B. Lewis calendar mechanism, ca. 1865, 31" h. **$1,500**

Gilbert Manufacturing Co. Maranville's patent octagon-drop calendar wall clock w/rosewood case & tablet bearing English royal crest, manufactured for British company N. C. Hyde and Co., ca. 1868, 24" h. **$600**.

William L. Gilbert Clock Co. "Admiral" eight-day time & calendar, octagon-drop school clock w/oak case, ca. 1901, 27 1/2" h. **$225**.

W. L. Gilbert "Office" walnut simple calendar octagon wall clock, applied decorations, eight-day time & strike, 32" h. **$1,200**.

W. L. Gilbert oak octagon calendar clock, time only, 18 x 28" h. **$595**.

Ingraham "Dew Drop" eight-day calendar
clock, ca. 1909, 23 1/2" h. **$200**.

Ingraham "Standard" eight-day calendar
clock, ca. 1909 24" h. **$235**.

Ingraham oak simple calendar wall clock
w/advertisement "R. Andreliunas Jeweler and
Music Dealer" on lower tablet, 16 x 36" h.
$850.

Ingraham oak simple calendar octagon wall clock, ca. 1910, face & tablet replaced w/exact copy, eight-day time only, 18 x 32" h. **$450.**

Ingraham walnut stained simple calendar wall clock w/calendar dates on upper dial, eight-day time only, 12 x 24" h. **$525.**

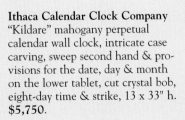

Ithaca Calendar Clock Company "Kildare" mahogany perpetual calendar wall clock, intricate case carving, sweep second hand & provisions for the date, day & month on the lower tablet, cut crystal bob, eight-day time & strike, 13 x 33" h. **$5,750.**

Ithaca Calendar Clock Company "No. 4 Hanging Office," rosewood case, 30-day, double-dial calendar clock, ca. 1880, 29" h. **$800.**

Close up of **Ithaca** "No. 4 Hanging Office" calendar dial.

Ithaca Calendar Company "No. 1" walnut perpetual calendar wall clock w/H. B. Horton's patents, April 18, 1865, & Aug. 28, 1866, & provisions for the date, day & month on the lower dial, sweep second hand, double weight driven, time only, 19 x 72" h. **$15,000.**

Ithaca Calendar Clock Company,
Horton's patent iron-case double-dial
perpetual calendar clock using
Hubbell's patented 30-day, time-only
pendulum movement, ca. 1866, 21" h.
$2,750.

Ithaca Calendar Clock Company
cast-iron ionic perpetual calendar
wall clock using H. B. Horton's
calendar movement as seen on
bottom dial, eight-day time only,
9 x 19" h. **$2,700.**

New Haven Clock Co. 8" lever-movement calendar wall clock, w/double-spring, ca. 1890, 11" h. **$210**.

Close up of back of **New Haven** 8" lever-movement calendar clock.

Oak octagon simple calendar clock, eight-day time & strike, late 1800s, 12 x 22" h. **$600**.

Sessions "Regulator E" eight-day, time & calendar store regulator, ca. 1908, 38 1/2" h. **$450**.

Sessions oak octagon short-drop calendar clock, time only, late 1800s, 18" x 20" h. **$595**.

Sessions walnut simple calendar wall clock, eight-day time only, ca. 1890, 39" h. **$550**.

Seth Thomas "Number 5" walnut perpetual calendar wall clock w/second hand, applied walnut decorations, calendar details found on lower dial, time only, weight driven, 50" h. **$7,500**.

Seth Thomas "Number 1" rosewood perpetual calendar wall clock, eight-day time only, weight driven, patented 1876, 40" h. **$3,750**.

Seth Thomas "Office Calendar No. 1," w/rosewood veneer, ca. 1868, 40" h. **$1,875**.

Seth Thomas "Office Number 11" mahogany perpetual calendar wall clock, eight-day time only, weight driven, patented 1876, 68 1/2" h. **$17,500**.

Waterbury "Calendar No. 33," oak case, double-dial, perpetual calendar clock, featuring eight-day movement w/hour & half-hour strike on cathedral gong, ca. 1900, 39 1/4" h. **$2,100**.

Waterbury "Calendar No. 36," oak case double-dial calendar clock, ca. 1891, 28" h. **$2,100**.

Waterbury eight-day, 12" drop-octagon calendar clock, w/rosewood veneered case & unusual bezel hinge at 12 o'clock, rather than at 3 or 9 o'clock, ca. 1895, 23" h. **$425**.

Waterbury oak octagon calendar wall clock w/long drop, features egg & dart molding, late 1800s, 15 x 30" h. **$695**.

E. N. Welch oak simple calendar wall clock, eight-day time only, ca. 1890, 18 x 40" h. **$695**.

Welch, Spring & Co. "Round Head Regulator No. 2" rosewood perpetual calendar wall clock w/provisions on the upper dial for the days of the week marked by a small hand & on the lower dial for the days indicated by a large hands & the months marked w/a small hand, Lewis patented calendar mechanism, eight-day time only, 13 x 34" h. **$1,600.**

Welch, Spring & Co., "Round Head Regulator No. 2," two-weight, double-dial calendar clock, ca. 1872, 34" h. **$1,000.**

A close-up of **B. B. Lewis's** perpetual calendar label patented Feb. 4, 1862, Sept. 15, 1863, June 21, 1864 & Dec. 20, 1864, on the Welch, Spring & Co. calendar clock.

Gallery Clocks

Ansonia walnut wall clock, eight-day time only, 9 1/2" d., fusee movement. **$1,500**.

E. Howard & Co., oak-case slave movement electric gallery clock w/18" dial, ca. 1920, 24" h. **$180**.

Seth Thomas walnut gallery clock, 15-day, time only, 18" dial, 25 1/2" outside d. **$2,500**.

Seth Thomas one-day lever-movement octagonal-case gallery clock, ca. 1885, 8 1/2" h. **$85**.

Seth Thomas one-day lever-movement 30-hour time & strike gallery clock w/rosewood veneer, ca. 1880, 13" h. **$275**.

Standard Electric Time Co., oak-case electric gallery clock w/24" dial, ca. 1915, 30 1/2" h. **$500**.

Waterbury "Oak Lever" eight-day octagonal-case gallery clock, ca. 1914, 10 7/8" h. **$100**.

Octagon Clocks

Ansonia Clock Co. "Office Regulator" eight-day time & strike, long-drop octagon clock w/black walnut case, ca. 1901, 32" h. **$525**.

Ansonia "Regulator A" walnut octagonal wall clock, w/ebony trim, eight-day time & strike, ca. 1900, 17 x 32" h. **$500**.

Ansonia oak, "Regulator B" drop octagon clock, time only, ca. 1890, 17 x 32" h. **$450**.

Ansonia oak miniature octagonal wall clock, time & strike, ca. 1910, 12 x 20" h. **$225.**

Atkins, Whiting & Co. 30-day wagon-spring-driven, drop-octagon clock w/ripple-molded rosewood veneer case, ca. 1855, 25" h. **$3,000.**

L. Hubbell 30-hour rosewood-veneer case octagon wall clock w/patent lever escapement, ca. 1870, 6" h. **$225.**

New Haven oak octagon wall clock w/short drop, eight-day time & strike, late 1800s, 17 x 24" h. **$425**.

New Haven eight-day time & strike, walnut-&-inlay case, long-drop school clock, ca. 1880, 32" h. **$420**.

Sessions oak octagon wall clock w/short drop, late 1800s, 16 x 25 1/2" h. **$395**.

Seth Thomas "Number 3" walnut octagon, long-drop wall clock, second hand, "Ball Watch Co., Cleveland" on dial, time only, weight driven, 14" dial, 44" h. **$4,500**.

Seth Thomas "Number 18" walnut octagon, long-drop wall clock, nickel-plated pendulum & weight, eight-day time only, weight driven, 14" dial, 54" h. **$4,000**.

Seth Thomas walnut octagon wall clock, 30-hour time only, 17 x 24" h. **$395**.

Seth Thomas walnut octagon wall clock, eight-day time & strike, ca. 1896, 15 x 22" h. **$375.**

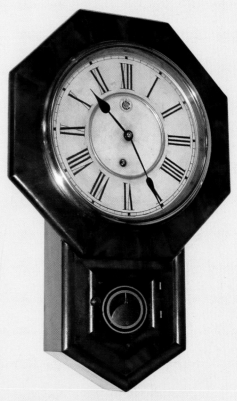

Waterbury "Drop Octagon, 10 Inch" eight-day mahogany-veneer clock, ca. 1895, 21 1/2" h. **$350.**

Seth Thomas walnut octagonal wall clock w/brass applied decorations, time only, ca. 1890, 16 x 25" h. **$375.**

Close up of label on **Waterbury** "Drop Octagon, 10 Inch" clock.

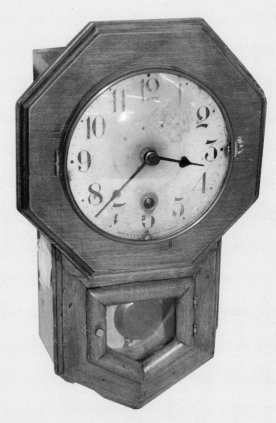

Waterbury oak octagon wall clock w/short drop, features egg & dart molding, late 1800s, 17 x 24" h. **$395**.

Waterbury octagon short-drop schoolhouse clock, 30-hour time only, 9 x 13" h. **$425**.

Waterbury oak octagon short-drop barbershop clock that show hands & face backwards, eight-day time only, 15" d. face, early 1900s, 8 x 22" h. **$2,500**.

Waterbury oak octagonal wall clock, eight-day time only, ca. 1900, 17 x 24" h. **$325**.

E. N. Welch "Gentry" eight-day, oak-case, short-drop octagon regulator, ca. 1900, 26" h. **$125**.

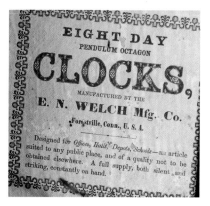

E. N. Welch "Verdi" rosewood octagon long-drop wall clock, eight-day time & strike, spring driven, ca. 1875, 31" h.; 11 1/2" dial. **$550**.

Close-up of label from **E. N. Welch** octagonal clock. The label reads, "Eight Day, Pendulum Octagon Clocks, Manufactured by the E. N. Welch Mfg. Co., Forestville, Conn., U.S.A. Designed for Offices, Halls, Depots, Schools—an article suited to any public place, and of quality not to be obtained elsewhere. A full supply, both silent and striking, constantly on hand."

Wall Regulator Clocks

Ansonia "Baghdad" oak wall clock, incised carving & applied decorations, special Ansonia silver etched glass, time only, double weight driven, 16 x 50" h. **$2,200.**

Ansonia "The Antique" model cabinet clock w/brass applied decorations, eight-day time & strike, 14 x 46" h. **$9,800.**

Ansonia "Antique Hanging" cherry wall clock, brass & porcelain dial, antique brass trimmings, eight-day time & strike, weight driven, 46 1/2" h. **$9,000.**

Ansonia "Queen Charlotte" oak wall clock, barley twist columns, pressed carving, eight-day time only, 16 x 42" h. **$950**.

Ansonia "Queen Elizabeth" oak wall clock, awarded a prize medal at the Paris Exposition in 1878 as indicated by the label on the back of the case, eight-day time & strike, 13 1/2 x 38" h. **$950**.

Ansonia "Queen Elizabeth" walnut wall clock, incised carving, eight-day time only, ca. 1901, 37" h. **$600**.

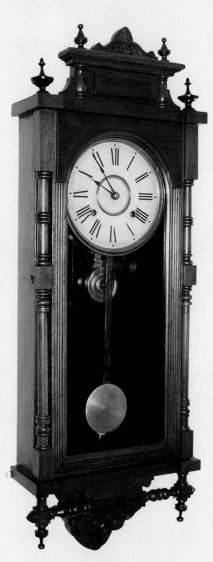

Ansonia "Queen Elizabeth" walnut wall clock, incised carving, eight-day time & strike, ca. 1901, 37" h. **$700**.

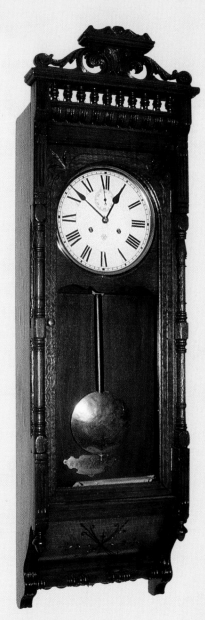

Ansonia "Santa Fe" oak wall clock w/two weights, eight-day time & strike, 15 x 53" h. **$2,200**.

Ansonia walnut short-drop wall clock,
30-day, time only, 11" dial, 24" h. **$350**.

Ansonia walnut two-weight wall
clock, eight-day time & strike,
late 1800s, 15 x 51" h. **$3,200**.

Eastman Clock Co., for Daniel Pratt's Son, Boston, Massachusetts, "Pendulum No. 1," eight-day weight-driven wall regulator clock, ca. 1895, 33" h. $1,600.

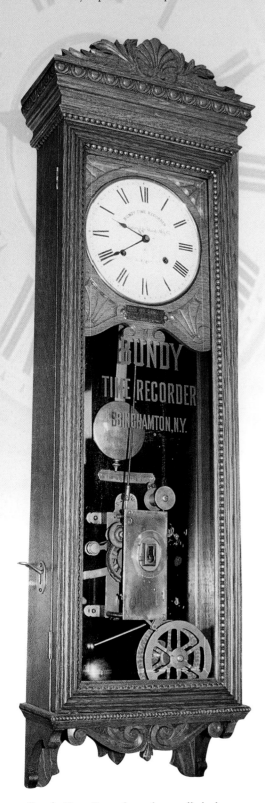

Bundy Time Recorder walnut wall clock, incised carving, runs 15 days, 16 x 55" h. The Bundy movement was by Seth Thomas. Each employee had a key number. $3,750.

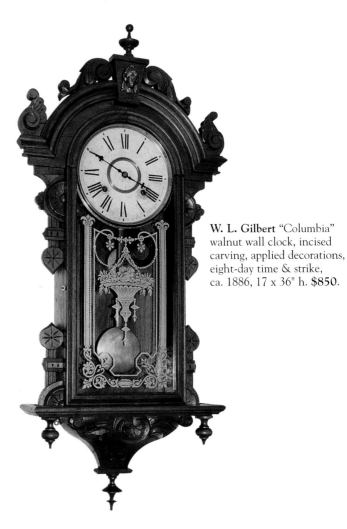

W. L. Gilbert "Columbia" walnut wall clock, incised carving, applied decorations, eight-day time & strike, ca. 1886, 17 x 36" h. $850.

W. L. Gilbert "Observatory" oak regulator wall clock, pressed designs & incised carving, eight-day time only, ca. 1910, 15 1/2 x 34" h. **$400**.

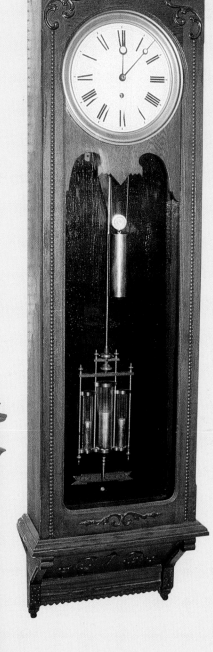

W. L. Gilbert oak jeweler's regulator wall clock, which once hung in the Marengo, Iowa, bank, eight-day time only, 18 x 72" h. **$6,900**.

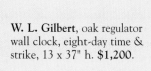

W. L. Gilbert, oak regulator wall clock, eight-day time & strike, 13 x 37" h. **$1,200**.

Ingraham oak wall clock w/steam-pressed designs on the case, eight-day time & strike w/alarm, late 1800s, 13 x 26" h. **$495**.

Chauncey Jerome wall clock, marked Bristol, Connecticut, 1840. Label reads: "Jerome & Co.'s Superior 8 day Anglo-American clocks, Home-use and Abroad." Eight-day time & strike, 17" d., 33" h. Hands missing. **$345**.

Ingraham walnut hanging kitchen wall clock, incised carving, thermometer & level attached to clock, eight-day time & strike, ca. 1893, 28" h. **$650**.

C. H. Maur wall clock, painted porcelain dial, ormolu face & hands, 15-jewel clock w/platform escapement, time only, 8 x 6 1/2" h. **$900.**

F. Kroeber walnut regulator wall clock, turned & reeded columns, sweep second hand, time only, weight driven, ca. 1898, 53" h. **$3,200.**

F. Kroeber "Jeweler's Regulator Number 58" brass lyre pendulum, sweep second hand, eight-day time only, pinwheel escapement (more desirable than the dead beat), 22 x 93" h. **$16,000.**

New Haven "Office Number 1" walnut regulator wall clock, second hand, time only, single-weight driven, ca. 1886, 42" h. **$1,200.**

New Haven oak wall clock, time & strike, chime rod rather than gong, ca. 1920, 16 x 31" h. **$475**.

New York Standard Watch Co. oak wall clock, originally run by a dry cell battery, patented Feb. 25, 1896, 20 x 48" h. **$1,595**.

New Haven mahogany wall clock, beveled glass, time & bimbam strike on two rods, ca. 1910, 8 x 24" h. **$275**.

Seth Thomas "Fine Regulator No. 10" walnut wall clock, mercury pendulum, sweep second hand, turned side columns, burl decorations, glass sides in top section, 14" silver dial, eight-day time only, 72" h. Some collectors consider this clock Thomas' best. **$30,000.**

Sessions "Regulator No. 5" walnut stained wall clock, incised carving, second hand, time only, double weight driven, ca. 1895, 20 x 49" h. **$3,700.**

Seth Thomas "Flora" oak wall clock, flower carved on clock's side, hand carving on case, eight-day time & strike, weight driven, 8" d. dial, 38" h. **$2,800.**

Seth Thomas "Eclipse" walnut wall clock, incised carving, eight day, time, strike, & alarm, Eclipse movement, ca. 1890, 15 x 27" h. **$600.**

Seth Thomas "Flora" walnut wall clock, incised designs & carving on side panel, eight-day time & strike, weight driven, ca. 1880, 13 x 38" h. **$2,600**.

Seth Thomas "Marcy" walnut wall clock, seen in 1884-1896 catalog, incised carving, eight-day time & strike, spring driven, 8 1/2" d. dial, 46" h. **$5,000**.

Seth Thomas "Number 1" rosewood regulator wall clock, round top, second hand, eight-day time only, weight driven, ca. 1855, 11" dial, 34" h. **$2,400**.

Seth Thomas "Number 1 Extra" walnut regulator, secondhand, time only, weight driven, ca. 1875, 13 1/2" dial, 40" h. **$2,750**.

Seth Thomas "Number 2" oak regulator wall clock, second hand, brass pendulum & weight, time only, weight driven, ca. 1900, 10 x 36" h. **$1,400**.

Seth Thomas "Number 60" mahogany regulator wall clock, brass pendulum & weight, eight-day time only, weight driven, 18 1/4 x 60" h. **$13,000**. (**$15,000** if mint.)

Seth Thomas "Number 60"
mahogany wall clock, sweep
second hand, brass weight,
eight-day time only, 14" dial,
58 1/2" h. **$15,000**.

Seth Thomas "Queen Ann"
oak wall clock, pictured in 1881
catalog, eight-day time & strike,
13 x 36" h. **$1,000**.

Seth Thomas "Regulator No. 5"
walnut wall clock (also called
"Miniature 16"), incised carving,
glass sides, porcelain dial, eight-day
time only, weight driven, 50" h.
$8,500.

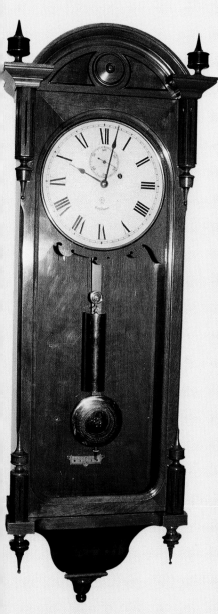

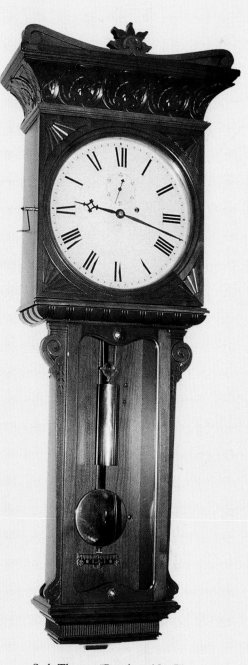

Seth Thomas "Regulator No. 6" walnut wall clock, second hand, brass weight & pendulum, eight-day time only, 10" d. dial, 49" h. The 1906 catalog lists this clock available in either mahogany or oak. **$4,000.**

Seth Thomas "Regulator No. 7" walnut wall clock, hand carved cabinet, brass weight & pendulum, secondhand, Graham deadbeat escapement, eight-day time only, ca. 1885, 19 x 48" h. **$11,000.**

Seth Thomas "Regulator No. 7" cherry wall clock, hand carved cabinet, Graham deadbeat escapement, cut steel pinion movement, second hand, eight-day time only, weight driven, 12" dial **$9,500.**

Seth Thomas "Regulator No. 8" cherry wall clock, second hand, brass weight & pendulum, eight-day time only, weight driven, 14" dial, 56" h. **$9,000**.

Seth Thomas "Regulator No. 19" walnut wall clock, incised carving, burl decorations, mercury pendulum, metal weight, Graham deadbeat escapement, second hand, eight-day time only, 23 x 77" h. **$20,000**.

Seth Thomas "Regulator No. 19" cherry wall clock, thumb spring mercury pendulum, sweep second hand, Graham deadbeat escapement, eight-day time only, weight driven, 23 x 75" h. **$22,000**.

Seth Thomas "Regulator No. 63" oak wall clock, applied decorations, beats seconds, Graham deadbeat escapement, eight-day time only, weight driven, ca. 1900, 14" dial, 76" h. **$12,000**.

Seth Thomas "Regulator No. 30" oak wall clock, incised carving, applied decorations, time only, weight driven, 18 x 48" h. **$2,200**.

Seth Thomas "Umbria" oak wall clock, second hand, brass pendulum, 15-day, time only, 40 1/2" h. **$1,600**.

Seth Thomas "Umbria" oak wall clock, 15-day, time only, double spring movement because of longer running time, 10" d. dial, 40 1/2" h. **$1,600**.

Seth Thomas walnut & burl-walnut wall clock, eight-day time & strike, 13 x 31" h. **$400**.

Seth Thomas walnut one-weight wall-hanging jeweler's regulator, ca. 1880, 23 1/2 x 67" h. **$5,200**.

Seth Thomas oak miniature regulator made for John Deere 150th anniversary in 1987, eight-day time only, 10 1/2 x 24" h. **$250**.

Seth Thomas walnut hanging kitchen wall clock, incised carving, thermometer & level attached to clock, eight-day time & strike, ca. 1890, 30" h. **$550**.

Unknown maker, miniature schoolhouse type, dark stained wall clock, time only, spring driven, patented 1920, 5" dial, 14 1/2" h. **$275**.

Unknown maker, hanging Victorian wall clock, porcelain & brass dial, bird on clock's top, time only, 8 x 20" h. **$350**.

Unknown maker, American made cabinet, jeweler's regulator, French works, walnut wall clock, pinwheel movement, time only, weight driven, ca. 1840 to 1850, 20 x 59" h. **$1,250**.

Waltham oak "16 Jewelers Regulator" wall clock, incised carving, time only, ca. 1895, 18 x 67" h. This clock hung in a Davenport, Iowa, jewelry store for 90 years $3,800.

Waterbury "Baha" gilded ionic wall clock, time & strike, ca. 1900, 13 x 21" h. $375.

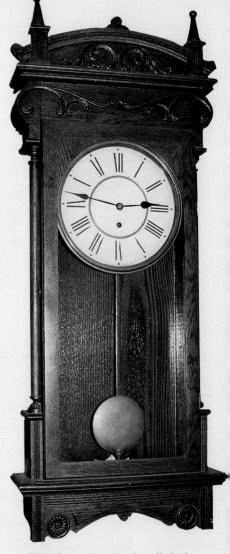

Waterbury "Cairo" oak wall clock, applied decorations, side columns, eight-day time only, 17 x 42" h. $650.

Waterbury "Number 53" walnut wall clock, eight-day time only, weight driven, ca. 1900, 20" w. at top, 53 1/4" h., 9" dial **$1,750**.

Waterbury "Para" rosewood ionic wall clock, time only, ca. 1891, 10" dial, 22" h. **$375**.

Waterbury cherry "Regulator No. 5" wall clock, burl decorations, incised carving, second hand, brass pendulum & weights, deadbeat escapement, second hand, glass sides, eight-day time & strike, 19 x 68" h. **$4,250**.

Waterbury "Union" walnut wall clock, pictured in its 1892 catalog, eight-day, spring driven **$500**.

Waterbury walnut wall clock, Eastlake-style, ca. 1890, 13 x 27" h. **$350**.

Waterbury oak regulator wall clock, secondhand, time only, weight driven, ca. 1912, 37" h. **$1,300**.

Waterbury oak regulator wall clock, eight-day time & strike, late 1800s, 15 x 40" h. **$1,095**.

Waterbury oak 30-day regulator time & strike, turn of century, 16 x 37" h. **$1,500.**

Waterbury oak two-weight wall clock, ca. 1880s, 15 x 36" h. **$2,900.**

Waterbury oak wall clock, eight-day time only, ca. 1880 to 1890, 16 x 39" h. **$895.**

Waterbury oak pillar-&-scroll two-weight wall clock w/exposed pendulum, trimmed w/brass sea horses, eight-day time & strike, 17 1/2 x 51" h. **$4,500.**

A close-up of the label that reads, "Alexis Thirty Day, Time Piece, Patent Escapement."

E. N. Welch "Alexis Number 1" rosewood ionic wall clock, 30-day movement, time only, 12" dial, 26" h. The dial has been removed to show the works **$500**.

E. N. Welch "Alexis Number 2" ebony decorated rosewood wall clock, applied gold leaf on tablet, eight-day time only, ca. 1875, 10" dial, 22" h. **$400**.

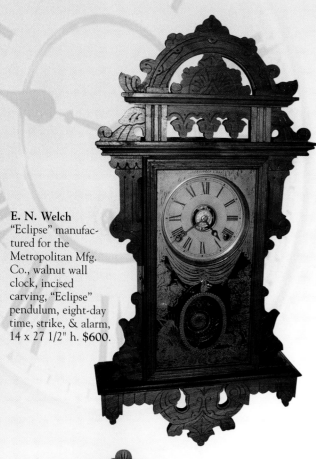

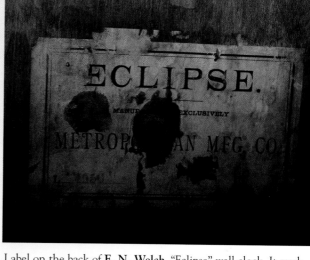

E. N. Welch "Eclipse" manufactured for the Metropolitan Mfg. Co., walnut wall clock, incised carving, "Eclipse" pendulum, eight-day time, strike, & alarm, 14 x 27 1/2" h. **$600**.

Label on the back of **E. N. Welch**, "Eclipse" wall clock. It reads, "Eclipse manufactured exclusively for Metropolitan Mfg. Co."

E. N. Welch "Hanging Italian" rosewood veneer w/walnut trim wall clock, Sandwich glass insert in pendulum seen to the left of the case, eight-day time & strike, 15 x 29" h. **$1,200**.

E. N. Welch "Meyerbeer" oak regulator wall clock (Meyerbeer was an Italian composer who wrote Torchlight March No. 1 in B flat), eight-day time & strike, ca. 1885, 14 x 40" h. **$800**.

E. N. Welch, "No. 11 Regulator"
mahogany wall clock, second hand,
incised carving, 30-day, time only,
spring driven, 18 x 60" h. **$3,500**.

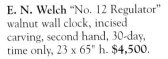

E. N. Welch "No. 12 Regulator"
walnut wall clock, incised
carving, second hand, 30-day,
time only, 23 x 65" h. **$4,500**.

E. N. Welch "Office Number 12"
oak wall clock, incised carving,
second hand, 30-day, time only,
ca. 1885, 23 x 65" h. **$3,750**.

E. N. Welch "Sembirch" walnut wall clock, incised carving, eight-day time only, ca. 1890, 14 x 39" h. **$700**.

E. N. Welch "Office 30-day" oak wall clock, incised carving, 30-day, time only, ca. 1900, 18 x 60" h. **$3,500**.

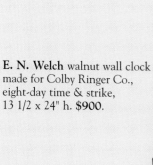

E. N. Welch walnut wall clock made for Colby Ringer Co., eight-day time & strike, 13 1/2 x 24" h. **$900**.

E. N. Welch walnut wall clock w/incised decorations, 30-hour time only, 15 x 36" h. **$350**.

E. N. Welch walnut wall clock (made exclusively for Metropolitan Mfg. Co., in New York), incised carving, painted dial, eight-day time, strike, & alarm, Eclipse pendulum, 14 x 27" h. **$650.**

Welch, Spring & Co. "No. 4 Regulator" walnut wall clock, turned columns, finials, deadbeat escapement, 30-day, time only, double spring driven, ca. 1880, 16 x 41" h. **$2,000.**

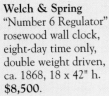

Welch & Spring "Number 6 Regulator" rosewood wall clock, eight-day time only, double weight driven, ca. 1868, 18 x 42" h. **$8,500.**

Welch, Spring & Co. "Number 4 Regulator" walnut wall clock, elaborately turned columns, upper finials, nickel-plated double spring movement, early model had wooden sides, later model had glass sides, 30-day time only, 1873-1884, 16 x 42" h. **$3,750.**

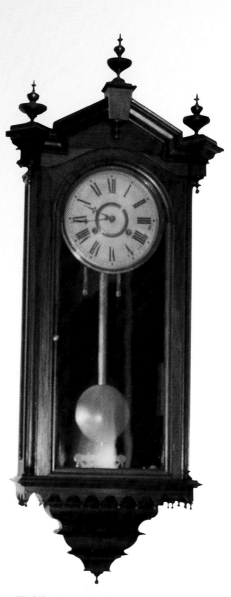

Welch, Spring & Co. "No. 4 Regulator" walnut wall clock, brass pendulum, deadbeat escapement, 30-day, time only, double spring driven, 15 x 42" h. **$1,900**.

Ken Williams walnut jeweler's regulator wall clock, eight-day time only, 25 to 30 years old, 21 x 85" h. **$3,200**.

Welch, Spring & Co. rosewood "Number 6 Regulator" or "Lucca Regulator," 1879-1884, w/two weights, movement has solid brass plates, lantern pinion & deadbeat escapement, eight-day time only, 18 1/2 x 42" h. **$7,200**.

Chapter 6
Classic Clocks

Four clock types fall into the "classic" category— the statue or figural clock, the crystal regulator, the porcelain shelf clock, and the cabinet clock.

All the original figural clocks manufactured in the United States were produced by the Ansonia Clock Company and included the "Arcadia," "Fortuna," "Gloria," and "Juno" models. They were eight-day, time-only, bronze-finished clocks with raised gold-plated numerals and ornamentation. Because there are known reproductions from European sources, buyers of these clocks should consult an expert to be sure their purchase is not a reproduction.

Commanding high prices on today's market is the crystal regulator, a clock with glass panels on four sides, exposing the works to full view. Its visible or open escapement and porcelain dial adds even more elegance to a beautiful timepiece. Crystal regulators can reach more than $3,000 in value.

The W. L. Gilbert Clock Company produced an unusual crystal regulator in about 1910 that stands on four fancy metal columns similar to an easel. The clock, finished in a rich ormolu gold,

Crystal Regulator Clocks

has a visible escapement and pendulum, and an ivory-colored porcelain dial.

One of Ansonia Clock Company's most expensive crystal regulators is the "Regal" clock, displayed in its 1906 catalog. Finished in rich gold or Syrian Bronze, the "Regal" featured an eight-day, half-hour gong striking movement, porcelain dial, visible escapement, and beveled glass on all sides. Today this clock sells for well over $4,000.

In a 1902 catalog, W. L. Gilbert presented a crystal regulator named "Verdi," with an eight-day, half-hour strike. It had an ivory dial, visible escapement, mercurial pendulum, and front, side, and back beveled-glass panels. Finished in a rich, ormolu gold, it cost $60.

A later catalog by Gilbert featured a crystal regulator called "Magdeleine." The case was made of rich Brazilian onyx with round, tapering onyx columns. The mountings were gold plate with heavy ornamental case decorations in a rich ormolu gold-plate finish. It was priced at $100; for an additional $3, a lion ornament could be added to the top.

The Waterbury Clock Company manufactured the "Paris" model crystal regulator. One of Waterbury's most expensive clocks of this type, the "Paris" sold for $50 in the early 1900s. Case finishes

Ansonia "Admiral" polished mahogany crystal regulator, finished in rich gold, porcelain dial, mercury pendulum, open escapement, beveled glass, eight-day time & half hour gong strike, 10 x 18" h. **$4,000.**

Ansonia "Apex" crystal regulator, finished in rich gold, porcelain dial, open escapement, beveled glass, eight-day time & strike, 10 x 19" h. **$3,600.**

included gold plate, Syrian bronze, polished brass, and polished mahogany. Other characteristics included an ivory dial, visible escapement, and beveled-glass front, sides, and back panels. It also had a cast gilt bezel.

Two unique crystal regulators in Seth Thomas' Empire line were named "Empire No. 31" and "Empire No. 32." Each had a bronze-finished girl's head on top of the clock.

Ansonia's china or porcelain shelf clocks were hand painted with gold decorations. They had a rack strike, as well as a strike on the half hour with a cathedral striking gong on a sounding board. Features such as a cream porcelain dial and a rococo sash made these clocks extremely desirable. Germany's Royal Bonn Company manufactured many of the porcelain cases for these clocks. They were decorated in rich colors—green, ruby, turquoise, cobalt blue, and violet. Other features on these clocks included a French or rococo sash, beveled glass panels, visible escapement, and a choice of Arabic or Roman numerals on the dial. While Royal Bonn made many of the cases, Ansonia produced most of the works for the clocks.

Clock advertisements used fancy phrases to depict a clock's charm. The following phrases from a catalog description exemplify this: "Assorted decorations, raised decorated flowers, Wedgwood decorations, rich color decorations, handpainted deco-

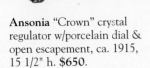

Ansonia "Crown" crystal regulator w/porcelain dial & open escapement, ca. 1915, 15 1/2" h. **$650.**

Ansonia "Elysian" eight-day time & strike crystal regulator, ca. 1914, 16 1/2" h. **$600.**

rations, floral design, richly decorated and tinted cases."

Statue clocks are another of Ansonia's contribution to the clock industry. The "Combatants" shows two warriors flanking the clock; "Pizarro and Cortez" presents a similar theme. "Music and Poetry" features two female artists, one on each side of the case.

Ansonia introduced a series of six cabinet clocks in the late 1800s called "Cabinet A," "Cabinet D," "Cabinet F," "Cabinet No. 1," "Cabinet Antique," and "Senator." They were made of mahogany, polished mahogany, antique oak, or polished oak, with brass or ormolu trimmings. They ranged from nineteen to twenty-three inches high. Today, the "Senator" is probably the most valuable. Its case is decorated with two antique brass female figures that flank the clock's dial.

Kroeber made more than fifty varieties of cabinet clocks. The clocks are spring driven with an eight-day time-and-strike movement. They range from thirteen-and-a-half to eighteen inches tall. The cases are made of ebony, mahogany, walnut, or ash and display four-and-one-half or five-inch dials. Kroeber's cabinet models date to the 1880s, and are identified by number ("Cabinet No. 3," "Cabinet No. 4," etc.) rather than by name.

Ansonia "Peer," eight-day time & strike crystal regulator, w/all brass case, ca. 1917, 12" h. **$535**.

Ansonia "Sovereign" polished mahogany crystal regulator, mercury pendulum, beveled glass, visible escapement, eight-day half-hour gong strike, 10 1/2 x 18 1/2" h. **$3,800**.

Ansonia crystal regulator, brass case, porcelain dial, & open escapement, eight-day time & strike, 7 1/2 x 8", 16" h. **$1,495**.

Ansonia polished-brass crystal regulator w/porcelain dial & open escapement, eight-day time & strike, 5 x 6 1/2", 10 3/4" h. **$600**.

Ansonia crystal regulator w/onyx top & base, visible (open) escapement, mercury pendulum, beveled plate glass, porcelain dial, eight-day half-hour gong strike, 10 x 17 1/4" h. **$4,000**.

Boston Clock Company "Alhambra" crystal regulator, patented Dec. 20, 1880, beveled glass, gold-plated case, 11-jeweled movement, porcelain dial, tandem wind movement, eight-day time & strike, 14 x 23 1/2" h. When new, cost was $133; now it is valued at **$4,000**.

Boston Clock Company "Crystal" eight-day time & strike crystal regulator w/Boston's tandem-wind, lever-escapement movement, ca. 1890, 9 3/4" h. **$500**.

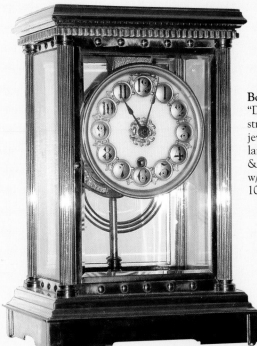

Boston Clock Company "Delphus" eight-day time & strike crystal regulator w/11-jeweled lever movement, porcelain dial, applied gilt numbers, & nickel-plated rear plates w/"damaskeen" finish, ca. 1890, 10 1/2" h. **$850**.

W. L. Gilbert crystal regulator w/brass case, porcelain face, & open escapement, eight-day time & strike, 7 x 8", 16" h. **$1,495**.

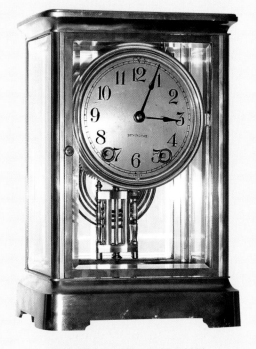

Seth Thomas "Empire No. 300" eight-day time & strike crystal regulator, ca. 1917, 9 1/2" h. **$250**.

Seth Thomas "Empire No. 65" bow-front crystal regulator, ca. 1909, 11" h. **$450**.

Seth Thomas "Orchid No. 4" eight-day crystal regulator. This is the only Seth Thomas model in which the top of the case is attached w/external screws that remain visible, ca. 1909, 10 3/4" h. **$250**.

Waterbury "Avignon" eight-day time & strike crystal regulator, ca. 1903, 17 1/2" h. **$550**.

Porcelain Clocks

Ansonia "La Cheze" Royal Bonn porcelain shelf clock, eight-day time & strike, 8 x 10" h. **$500**.

Ansonia "La Clair" Royal Bonn porcelain shelf clock, porcelain dial, rococo sash on door, eight-day time & strike, ca. 1890, 9 1/2 x 13" h. **$650**.

Ansonia "La Marine" Royal Bonn porcelain shelf clock w/open escapement, eight-day time & strike, 12 x 12" h. **$1,000**.

Ansonia "La Orb" Royal Bonn porcelain shelf clock, eight-day time & strike, 14 x 13" h. **$1,000**.

Ansonia "La Orne" Royal Bonn porcelain shelf clock, porcelain dial, eight-day time & strike, ca. 1890, 12 x 11" h. **$700**.

Ansonia "La Vinda" porcelain shelf clock w/open escapement, eight-day time & strike, 14 x 11" h. **$1,100**.

Ansonia "La Vinda" Royal Bonn porcelain shelf clock w/open escapement & decorative brass surround, eight-day time & strike, late 1800s, 14 x 11" h. **$900**.

Ansonia "Porcelain J" porcelain shelf clock, time only, ca. 1895, 6 x 12" h. **$300**.

Ansonia "Potomac" porcelain shelf clock, eight-day time & strike, ca. 1895, 13 1/2 x 11" h. **$850**.

Ansonia "Review" porcelain shelf clock w/open escapement, eight-day time & strike, 12 1/2 x 11" h. **$825**.

Ansonia "Romance" porcelain shelf clock w/open escapement, eight-day time & strike, 13 x 11" h. **$600**.

Ansonia "Winnipeg" porcelain shelf clock, eight-day time & strike, 10 x 12" h. **$450**.

Ansonia porcelain shelf clock, turn of century, eight-day time & strike, 18 x 19" h. **$1,800**.

Ansonia Royal Bonn porcelain shelf clock w/open escapement, patented June 14, 1881, eight-day time & strike, 14 x 14" h. **$950**.

Ansonia porcelain shelf clock, 30-hour, 5 x 7" h. **$100**.

Ansonia porcelain shelf clock, eight-day time & strike, 10 x 9" h. **$400**.

Ansonia porcelain shelf clock
w/German case, eight-day time
& strike, 9 1/2 x 9" h. **$450**.

Ansonia porcelain
mantel clock, eight-day
time & strike, 10 x 10" h.
$695.

Ansonia porcelain shelf clock
under glass dome, eight-day time
& strike, ca. 1890 to 1900,
14 x 17" h. **$2,250**.

Ansonia porcelain shelf clock
without glass dome.

Ansonia porcelain shelf clock w/open escapement, 10 1/2 x 17" h. **$1,500**.

California Porcelain Company shelf clock, 30-hour, ca. 1950, 6 x 8" h. **$89**.

Aradora porcelain snail-design shelf clock, early 1900s, 5 1/2 x 4 1/2" h. **$65**.

W. E. Gilbert porcelain shelf clock,
eight-day time & strike, late 1800s,
11 x 10 1/2" h. **$900**.

W. M. Gilbert porcelain mantel clock, eight-day
time & strike, early 1900s, 13 x 12" h. **$190**.

Jennings Brothers porcelain shelf clock w/eye cup
at base, time only, early 1900s, 7 1/2 x 8" h. **$150**.

Kroeber "China 31" shelf clock w/eclipse movement made by Seth Thomas, eight-day time & strike, 11 x 18" h. **$600**.

Kroeber "China 32" eclipse-movement shelf clock, 11 x 17 1/2" h. **$550**.

View of eclipse movement used in "China 31" & "China 32" clocks.

New Haven porcelain shelf clock, eight-day time & strike, early 1900s, 7 1/2 x 11" h. **$595**.

New Haven "Thistle" porcelain hanging wall clock, w/brass surround & wall chain, 15-day, time only, 10 x 14" h. **$650**.

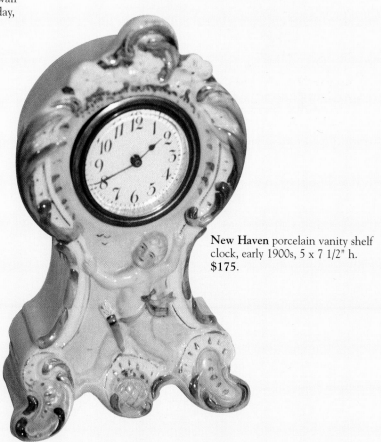

New Haven porcelain vanity shelf clock, early 1900s, 5 x 7 1/2" h. **$175**.

New Haven porcelain shelf clocks w/blue & white delft colors, 7 1/2" to 10" h. **$250 each**.

New Haven porcelain hanging wall clock, patented July 1895, secondhand, eight-day time only, 7" d. **$300**.

Porcelain shelf clock, eight-day time & strike, 9 x 12", 22" h. **$2,200**.

Porcelain shelf clocks: left, Ansonia showing baby w/clock; middle, German-made colored green & white; right, New Haven, colored green & white, ca. 1900, 6" to 8" height range, **$250-275 each**.

Porcelain vanity clock w/two birds sitting on clock frame, 14 x 9 1/2" h. **$85**.

Porcelain vanity shelf clock, 5 1/2 x 8" h. **$185**.

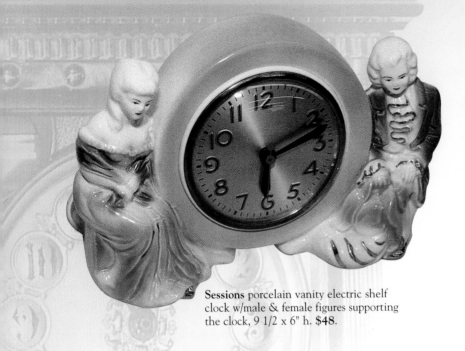

Sessions porcelain vanity electric shelf clock w/male & female figures supporting the clock, 9 1/2 x 6" h. **$48**.

Waterbury wall clock, patented 13 Jan. 1891, 30-hour time only, 8 x 10" h. **$300**.

Waterbury "Parlor Number 98" porcelain shelf clock, porcelain dial, eight-day time & strike, nickel-plated movement, 9 x 11" h. **$450**.

S t a t u e / F i g u r a l   C l o c k s

Ansonia "Crystal Palace Number 1"
w/two figures under glass dome,
mercury pendulum, time & strike,
15 x 19" h. **$1,800**.

Ansonia "Arcadia" swing stature or figural clock,
factory finished bronze & nickel, originally made for
jewelry store windows as attention getters, eight-day
time only, 4 1/2" dial, 3 1/2" h. **$5,250**.

Ansonia "Fantasy" statue clock, ca. 1890,
porcelain dial, open escapement, bronze
finish, French rococo sash, eight-day time
& strike, 17 1/2 x 14" h. **$800**.

Ansonia "Florida Group" statue
clock of two girls w/bird & flowers,
open escapement, chartreuse dial,
ormolu trimmings, eight-day time &
strike, 12 x 36" h. **$5,000**.

Ansonia "Gloria" swing statue or
figural clock, barbedienne bronze
finish, gold numbers on dial &
gilded pendulum, eight-day time,
4 1/2 x 28 1/2" h. **$5,500**.

Ansonia "Fortuna" swing statue or figural
clock, original bronze finish w/gilt pendulum,
eight-day time, 4 1/2" dial, 30" high. **$5,500**.

Ansonia "Hermes" statue clock, porcelain dial, eight-day time & strike, ca. 1895, 16 x 15" h. On the original clocks, the buyer had a choice of three different finishes: Japanese Bronze, Syrian Bronze, or Barbedienne. **$700.**

Ansonia "Juno" swing statue or figural clock, bronze finish, gilded pendulum, eight-day time, 4 1/2" dial, 28" h. **$4,000.**

Ansonia "Music" model iron statue clock w/marble bottom, brass decorations, & open escapement. **$2,195.**

Ansonia "Olympia" statue clock, bronze finish, beveled glass, porcelain dial, balance wheel escapement, eight-day time & strike, 15 1/2 x 24 1/2" h. **$1,800**.

Ansonia "Pizarro" statue clock, original Japanese bronze finish, porcelain dial, visible escapement, beveled glass, rococo sash, eight-day time & strike, 19 1/2 x 21 1/2" h. **$1,600**.

Ansonia "Shakespeare" statue clock, porcelain dial, open escapement, bronze finish, French rococo sash, beveled glass, eight-day time & strike, half hour gong, 17 1/2 x 15" h. **$750**.

Ansonia "Undine and Gloria" statue clock of girl w/harp & wings. "Undine" is the name of the base & "Gloria" is the name of the statue. Porcelain dial, original finish, eight-day time & strike, 16 x 28" h. **$3,000**.

Ansonia "Sibyl & Winter" statue clock w/two cupids on base, original finish, eight-day time & strike, 16 3/4 x 27" h. **$2,900**.

Ansonia "Summer and Winter" statue clock w/a bronze finish, porcelain dial, open escapement, French rococo sash, beveled glass, eight-day time & strike, w/half hour gong, 24 x 22" h. **$4,750**.

Ansonia cast-iron statue clock w/open escapement, eight-day time & strike, 21 x 16" h. **$1,495**.

Ansonia novelty statue clock w/croquet players, brass & porcelain dial, French rococo sash, patented April 28, 1876, time only, 8 x 7 1/2" h. **$300**.

Ansonia statue shelf clock w/fisherman & hunter figures, double mercury style pendulum, 14 x 15" h. **$700**.

Commerce Clock Co. iron statue clock w/gild coating, 30-hour time only, 10 1/2 x 13" h. **$110**.

W. L. Gilbert "Beatrice" w/harp statue clock w/bronze finish, mercury pendulum, open escapement, French rococo sash, eight-day time & strike, 13" h. **$1,400**.

W. L. Gilbert "Mignon" statue clock, shown in their 1900 trade catalog, gilt finished case, statue & feet, porcelain dial, nickel-plate movement, marbleized base, all original, seven-day, time & strike **$575**.

F. Kroeber "Noiseless Rotary No. 2" statue clock of a woman w/parasol sitting on top of a black enameled mantel clock. Patented June 18, 1878, when Kroeber was located at No. 14 Cortlandt Street (old Number 8) New York, eight-day time & strike, 9 1/2 x 22" h. **$1,750.**

W. L. Gilbert statue clock of a cupid stringing his bow, brass decorations & two cherubs at base, open escapement, porcelain dial, eight-day time & strike, 10 x 33" h. **$3,000.**

W. L. Gilbert statue clock, porcelain dial, metal & bronze clock & bronze figure at side w/marbleized wooden base & cast feet, eight-day movement, ca. 1900, 14 1/2 x 14" h. **$500.**

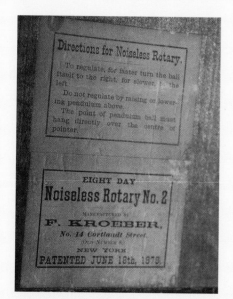

Label from F. Kroeber "Noiseless Rotary No. 2." Directions for Noiseless Rotary: "To regulate, for faster turn the ball itself to the right, for slower, to the left. Do not regulate by raising or lowering pendulum above. The point of pendulum ball must hang directly over the center of pointer."

Kroeber "Umbria" statue clock w/brass feet & cast-iron body, eight-day time & strike, 13 x 16 1/2" h. **$350.**

F. Kroeber statue clock of bowman, eight-day time & strike, spring driven, 15 x 23" h., **$950.**

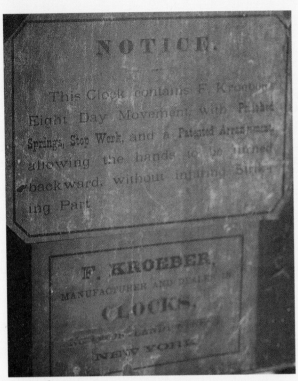

Label from **F. Kroeber's** statue clock reading, "This Clock contains F. Kroeber's Eight Day Movement w/Polished Springs, Stop Work, and a Patented Arrangement allowing the hands to be turned backward, without injuring Striking Part. F. Kroeber, manufacturer and dealer in clocks."

Seth Thomas "The Whistler" gilt finished statue clock, eight-day time, 14" h. **$900**.

Metal statue for clock, 9 x 9" h. **$65**.

Seth Thomas & Sons "No. 8028" statue clock w/work by Mitchell, Vance & Co. of a lady sitting on a throne playing a harp, eight-day time & strike, ca. 1880 to 1890, 14 x 18" h. **$1,200**.

Unknown maker, Spanish American War iron front statue clock w/bronze finish, time only, 10 x 11" h. **$235**.

Unknown maker, "Father Time" American brass finished statue clock, wall mounted, patented Sept. 22, 1885, time only, 10 x 11" h. **$275**.

Warner cupid iron front statue clock, porcelain face, bronze finish w/cupid holding up the clock, time only, dated May 15, 1906, 6 x 9 1/2" h. **$150.**

Waterbury & Canadian boudoir metal statue clocks, gilded finish, time only; left, Waterbury w/buffalo, center, Canadian w/child holding the clock, right, Waterbury, 5 1/2" to 9" h. **$150 each.**

Cabinet Clocks

Ansonia "Cabinet Antique Number 1" polished mahogany shelf clock, antique brass trimmings, porcelain & brass dial, eight-day time & half hour, Old English bell strike, ca. 1896, 11 1/2 x 18 3/4" h. **$4,000**.

Ansonia "Cabinet Antique" polished mahogany cabinet clock w/antique brass trimmings, French sash, finials, porcelain & brass face, eight-day time & strike, 9 1/4 x 20" h. **$2,800**.

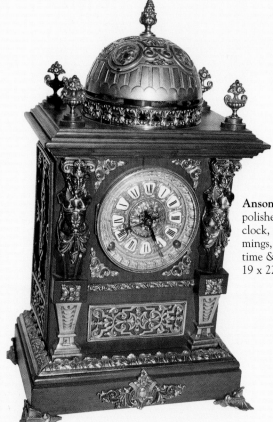

Ansonia "The Senator" polished mahogany cabinet clock, antique brass trimmings, silver dial, eight-day time & half hour gong strike, 19 x 22" h. **$4,000**.

Chapter 7
Shelf Clocks

The shelf clock was probably the first type of clock that fit easily into most homes. A table, shelf, or mantel was all that was needed to display this clock. Also, it could be produced more cheaply and easily than the bulkier tall-case clocks. Before the introduction of shelf clocks, the clockmaker and his apprentice or apprentices made clocks one at a time. Handcrafted methods required an inordinate amount of time to make a clock and, consequently, limited the quantity that could be manufactured. But when waterpower became more readily available to run machinery, production volume increased.

When clocks were no longer made one at a time to fill individual orders, a new method of marketing was needed. Because retail stores could only sell small numbers of the manufactured clocks, clockmakers often became itinerant merchants or hired peddlers to sell their surplus supplies. In general, clock cases were omitted to reduce cost to customers, as well as the weight the peddlers had to carry. Because all the essential parts were there, customers could hang up the clocks as they were or have cases custom made.

Alarm Clocks

Four forms of shelf clocks took over the market during the last quarter of the nineteenth century. Parlor clocks, made primarily of walnut, prevailed from around 1870 to 1900; "blacks" (black mantel clocks) were in favor from 1880 to just before 1920; oaks or kitchen clocks, mass produced by the millions, achieved their popularity from 1890 until well into the 1900s; and alarms were in vogue from 1875. These alarms were the earliest mechanical clocks and were used in monasteries by the monks to keep their appointments. They lacked dials and simply sounded a bell to awaken the monk.

Clock cases were made of wood, with mahogany the favorite. However, clockmakers were looking for other materials. Their new creations included iron cases, painted cases with Oriental designs, papier mâché with mother-of-pearl inlay, and early plastic celluloid, which was patented in 1869. It was not until the early 1900s, however, that celluloid clocks

Ansonia, left, "Amazon" alarm clock, 5" dial **$150**. Ansonia, right, alarm clock, 5" dial **$150**.

Three alarms. Left, advertising clock for Muscatine, Iowa radio station KTNT **$50**. Center, Big Ben eight-day alarm advertising Geo. H. Alps, Jeweler & House Furnisher, Burlington, Iowa **$65**. Right, chicken on dial advertising Cruso H. S. B. & Co. **$50**.

appeared on the market. The majority of these were small, thirty-hour, time-only shelf clocks.

The Western Clock Company, established in La Salle, Illinois, in 1895, manufactured two well-known varieties of alarm clocks—the "Big Ben," introduced in 1910, and the "Little Ben" in 1915. Today these clocks are produced by Westclox, which became the company name in 1936.

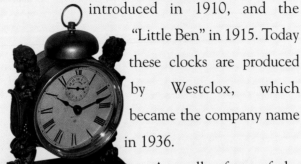

A smaller form of the Connecticut shelf clock was the cottage clock, first made in the late 1800s. Most examples have thirty-hour movements and wooden cases that are usually less than one foot in height, with flat or three-sided tops. Most were made in the last quarter of the nineteenth century.

Ansonia left, "Snap" alarm clock w/dog beneath clock, 8 3/4" h. **$400.** Right, Ansonia "Pride" alarm clock w/figures flanking clock, ca. 1880, 7 1/2" h. **$425.**

The Ansonia Clock Company developed a novel shelf timepiece called the inkstand clock. It usually had two ink containers flanking the central clock and was six to thirteen inches high. It was usually one day, time only, and sometimes had a simple calendar attached. Two of Ansonia's clocks are named "Parlor Ink Stand No. 2" and "Office Ink Stand." Nicholas Muller's Sons & Company also produced inkstand clocks. Several of their clocks were offered with an optional call bell on top. Often, the ink bottles were made of cut glass.

A unique type of shelf clock appeared in the

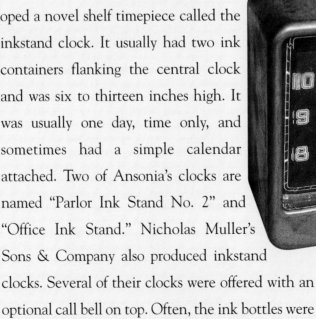

Ansonia Improved Square Simplex iron-case alarm clock, 4 1/2 x 5 1/2" h. **$45.**

middle 1800s. It was made of papier mâché, which was mashed paper mixed with glue and other adhesive materials, and could be easily molded. Decorations, such as mother-of-pearl and its imitations, were sometimes added to the finished product. Credited with being the largest producer of this type of clock was the Litchfield Manufacturing Company of Litchfield, Connecticut. Otis & Upson Company of Marion, Connecticut, was also known to have produced these cases. After these clocks caught the public's attention, a substitute was introduced called "iron mâché," which was produced using a painting and gilding process to make cast-iron-front clocks look like genuine papier mâché models.

The Jerome Company produced a large series of papier mâché shelf clocks. For their age, they are reasonably inexpensive. Another unique manufactured clock was the pearl-inlaid style that had model names such as "Jenny Lind," "LaFayette," "Union," and "Washington," which gave the clocks a patriotic feel.

Elias Ingraham of Bristol, Connecticut, is credited with designing the steeple clock with its pointed Gothic style. Steeple clocks were produced around 1840 when brass-coiled springs became available after clockmakers developed an interest in inexpensive brass-movement clocks. The clocks have two or four steeples and measure between ten-and-a-half and twenty-four inches high, with two in-between sizes of fourteen-and-three-quarter

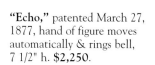

"Echo," patented March 27, 1877, hand of figure moves automatically & rings bell, 7 1/2" h. **$2,250**.

New Haven "Beacon" alarm clock in original box, 4 1/2 x 6" h. **$125**.

inches and twenty inches. The smallest steeples have been called sub miniatures. Steeple clocks are still made today.

When Elisah C. Brewster and Elias and Andrew Ingrahams were in partnership in the early 1800s, one of their advertisements read as follows: "Have constantly on hand, at their factory in Bristol, Conn., their various styles of patent spring eight-day and thirty-hour brass clocks, in mahogany, zebra, rosewood, and black walnut cases."

Connecticut shelf clocks were popular commodities from the late 1840s until the early 1900s. One of these clocks, the beehive, which has a rounded Gothic arch, resembled the inverted hull of a ship. Its average size was eleven inches wide and eighteen-and-a-half inches high. Most clockmakers produced this popular clock.

Decorating clock tablets was an easy task in the nineteenth century because hundreds of stencil patterns were available. By the late 1800s, clock tablets with decalcomania transfers (decals) could easily be purchased. These patterns, however, were not as desirable as the reversed-painted ones. Etched glass examples appeared after 1840, but most were used on better clocks.

In the late 1800s, the Ansonia Clock Company offered a group of three oak shelf clocks for a discount price of $12.60. They were eight-day clocks named "Gallatin," "Echo," and "Griswold." Ansonia claimed that the gong-strike clocks would

New Haven "Giant" alarm clock, 5" dial **$150.**

New Haven leather travel alarm clock, 4 x 4 1/2", 4" h. **$3.**

be sure sellers and big money makers.

Seth Thomas, in an attempt to outdo the other clock companies, produced a series of clocks that were named after American and international cities. They were all spring-driven, eight-day, time-and-strike clocks, available with walnut, rosewood, or oak cases. The four international clocks in the series were the "Athens," "Cambridge," "Oxford," and "Rome" models. The American clocks models were the "Atlanta," "Boston," "Buffalo," "Detroit," "Newark," "New York," "Omaha," "Peoria," "Pittsburgh," "Santa Fe," "St. Paul," "Tacoma," and "Topeka."

In the 1880s, the New Haven Clock Company developed a series of eight-day time-and-strike, walnut-case mantel clocks named after world rivers. Some of the names selected were the "Danube," "Rhine," "Seine," "Thames," "Tiber," and "Volga."

Not to be outdone, the W. L. Gilbert Clock Company joined what seemed to be a clock-series competition. Gilbert developed a line of fish and animal timepieces around 1891. The clocks had eight-day movements and were finished in either oak or walnut. The cases were named after six species of fish: bass, carp, pike, salmon, shark, and trout, and were all about twenty-two inches tall. The animal cases, featuring the buffalo, hyena, leopard, lion, panther, and tiger, were about twenty-one inches tall.

Parker Clock Co. alarm clock w/brass statue of a girl carrying a basket, 30 hour, time and alarm, 7 x 13" h. **$900**.

Phinney–Wallace portable alarm clock, early 1900s, 4 1/2 x 4" h. **$20**.

The Welch, Spring and Company developed a series of clocks that were named after theater and opera artists. One of the most well known was Adelina Patti, an opera prima donna.

Some of the clock series featured images of historical figures at the top of the case. These famous people included Admiral Dewey (produced by Ingraham and Welch), President McKinley (produced by Ingraham), and Admiral Schley (produced by Welch). Manufacturers customarily placed ten- by twelve-inch labels on the inside backboard of the cases. The type of clock, the maker, and the location were listed on the center of the label, and the phrase, "Warranted if Well Used" was almost always included.

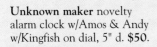

Unknown maker novelty alarm clock w/Amos & Andy w/Kingfish on dial, 5" d. $50.

Larger clock companies produced oak clocks (kitchen clocks) in large numbers, with Ingraham ranking as the highest producer. The pressed design on many of the oak shelf clocks was created by a rotary press that forced the design into the wood after it had been softened with steam. The kitchen clocks were typically twenty-three inches tall, had substantial eight-day, longwearing striking movements, and featured a glass-panel tablet decorated in bronze or silver gilt. Their $4 to $6 price tag enabled many American homes to display them. They remained popular from the late 1800s to about 1915. During this time, millions of the inexpensive clocks were manufactured.

Unknown maker, advertising Jordan Jeweler & Optician, Davenport, Iowa, on dial $75.

Mantel clock assortments were also offered at reasonable prices. A special carload buy of six highly embossed oak cases with E. Ingraham movements was listed at $8.20.

An advertisement read, "Our imitation French marble clocks are a reproduction of the French designs in wood, HIGHLY POLISHED, nicely engraved and gilded. We guarantee the finish on these cases to stand equal to any iron case on the market."

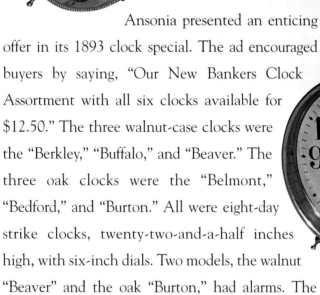

Unknown maker, left, alarm clock advertising McCabe Jewelers, Rock Island, Illinois, on dial **$70**. **Unknown maker**, right, alarm clock advertising Frank the Jeweler, Muscatine, Iowa, on dial **$60**.

Ansonia presented an enticing offer in its 1893 clock special. The ad encouraged buyers by saying, "Our New Bankers Clock Assortment with all six clocks available for $12.50." The three walnut-case clocks were the "Berkley," "Buffalo," and "Beaver." The three oak clocks were the "Belmont," "Bedford," and "Burton." All were eight-day strike clocks, twenty-two-and-a-half inches high, with six-inch dials. Two models, the walnut "Beaver" and the oak "Burton," had alarms. The shipping case was provided, but the customer had to buy all six clocks.

Unknown maker, advertising Paul's Jewelry Co., Burlington, Iowa, time & alarm **$75**.

Because of the shortage of black walnut, which had been used extensively for clock cases, marbleized or black mantel clocks called "blacks" became popular around 1880. They were made of marble, black iron, or black enameled wood. Many of the clocks were elaborately engraved and inlaid, and added brass ornamentation gave them extra character. An early century Sears Roebuck catalog suggested using sweet oil to keep their finish clean.

In company with the mantel clocks were the tambour clocks, which had rounded tops and were often called "camelbacks" or "hunchbacks." This style was introduced at the beginning of the twentieth century and is still being produced today.

Seth Thomas used an exclusive coating on his mantel and tambour clocks called adamantine finish. The finish, extremely hard and durable, provided wooden clocks with a perfect imitation of marble. Major clock catalogs featured the black enamel wood clocks and described them as "Finished to imitate Italian marble and green Mexican onyx." An E. Ingraham Company trade catalog stated, "Our imitation French marble clocks are a reproduction of the French designs in wood, HIGHLY POLISHED, nicely engraved and gilded. We guarantee the finish of these cases to stand equal to any iron case on the market."

Missing clock parts can readily be acquired today from companies that produce hands, dials, finials, and other small clock parts. They also sell bronze statues that were top pieces for clocks and can take the place of damaged or missing ones. Some collectors do not make changes, but keep their clocks in as near their original condition as possible. If parts are replaced, however, it is best to keep the originals.

Unknown maker, advertising Quincy on dial, patented 1907, dual alarm $75.

Unknown maker, grandfather's moon dial, time & alarm, 6" h. $1,500.

Unknown maker, double bell Snoopy alarm clock, 3 1/2" d. $25.

Westclox Big Ben advertising C. G. Samuelson Jeweler, Orion, Illinois, on dial **$75**.

Westclox Big Ben alarm clock w/black face, 5" d., **$125**.

Westclox Baby Ben made by Western Clock Co., LaSalle, Illinois, patent number, 1,563,4321 (1924), 3" d. **$65**.

Westclox Baby Ben alarm clock, late 1900s, 3 1/2" d. **$25**.

Westclox alarm clock, 20th c., 5 x 5 1/2" h. **$25**.

Westclox walnut vanity alarm clock, early 1900s, 4 1/2 x 4 1/2" h. **$20**.

Westclox identical brass metal alarm clocks w/different finishes, 4 x 5 1/2" h. **$125 each**.

Black Mantel Clocks

Ansonia "Belgium" cast-iron, black enameled mantel clock, porcelain dial, dragons on each end, eight-day time & strike, ca. 1890, 18 x 12" h. **$400**.

Ansonia "Boston Extra" cast-iron black enameled mantel clock, porcelain dial, open escapement, green pillars, eight-day time & strike, ca. 1890, 15 x 11 1/2" h. **$350**.

Ansonia "Capri" cast-iron, black enameled mantel clock, porcelain dial, open escapement, eight-day time & strike, ca. 1890, 15 x 12" h. **$350**.

Ansonia "Carlisle" cast-iron, black enameled mantel clock, gilded pillars, lion heads & feet, eight-day time & strike, ca. 1901, 17 x 10" h. **$200**.

Ansonia "Denmark" cast-iron, black enameled mantel clock, gold tinted face, three marbleized columns on each side, eight-day time & strike, ca. 1890, 16 1/2 x 12" h. **$500**.

Ansonia "La France" cast-iron, black enameled mantel clock, brass sunburst dial, gilded decorations, eight-day time & strike, ca. 1890, 11 1/2 x 11" h. **$200**.

Ansonia "Lisle" cast-iron, black enameled mantel clock, gilt-applied decorations, eight-day time & strike, ca. 1890, 11 x 10 1/2" h. **$300**.

Ansonia "London Extra" cast-iron, black enameled mantel clock, brass sunburst dial, gilded pillar & lion heads, eight-day time & strike, ca. 1895, 11 1/2 x 12 1/2" h. **$300.**

Ansonia "Montague" cast-iron, black enameled mantel clock, porcelain face, gilded decorations, eight-day time & strike, ca. 1890, 13 x 12" h. **$300.**

Ansonia "Rosalind" cast-iron mantel clock w/black enamel finish, porcelain dial, gilded decorations, seated lady on top, eight-day time strike, ca. 1890, 15 x 19" h. **$650.**

Label on back of **Ansonia** mantel clock. Unusual to have label on this type of clock. It reads, "Prize medal awarded Paris Exposition, 1878..."

Ansonia "Unique" black enameled metal case mantel clock, slate dial, gilded decorations, eight-day time & strike, ca. 1890, 9 1/2 x 10" h. **$250**.

Ansonia cast-iron, black enameled mantel clock, porcelain dial, open escapement, applied gilded decorations, eight-day time & strike, ca. 1890, 13 x 10" h. **$400**.

Ansonia cast-iron, black enameled mantel clock, slate dial, open escapement, four marbleized columns & trim, eight-day time & strike, ca. 1890, 16 x 13" h. **$500**.

Ansonia plush mantel clock, flush dial, beveled glass, gilded winged dragon feet & lion heads, eight-day time & strike, ca. 1895, 10 1/2 x 12 3/4" h. **$300**.

Ansonia iron-case shelf clock, time & strike w/half-hour strikes, ca. 1890s, 7 1/2 x 14" h. **$425**.

Ansonia metal-case mantel clock, eight-day time & strike, 15 x 12" h. **$360**.

Ansonia black marble shelf clock w/gilded decorations, eight-day, 11 1/2 x 10" h. **$225**.

W. L. Gilbert "Curfew" Italian marble finish mantel clock, eight-day time & strike, ca. 1910, 16 x 17 1/2" h. **$375**.

W. L. Gilbert black wooden-case mantel clock w/gilded decorations, eight-day time & strike, strikes on hour & half-hour, ca. 1900, 17 x 11" h. **$185**.

Ingraham black-iron mantel clock w/four marbleized pillars, brass feet, & body decorations, eight-day time & strike, 17 x 11" h. **$295**.

Ingraham black mantel clock, eight-day, ca. 1880, 14 1/2 x 9 1/2" h. **$225**.

Ingraham wooden-case mantel clock w/marbleized columns & copper applied decorations, 16 x 12" h. **$195**.

Mantel clock w/black adamantine-finished wooden case, maker may be Seth Thomas, eight-day time & strike, 19 x 11" h. **$300**.

New Haven wooden-case black mantel clock, eight-day, ca. 1900, 14 1/2 x 10 1/2" h. **$195**.

Sessions cast-iron, black enameled mantel clock, gilded pillars, lion heads & feet, 15 1/2 x 10 1/2" h. **$225**.

Sessions cast-iron, black enameled mantel clock, gilded decorations & feet, eight-day time & strike, 15 x 10" h. **$175**.

Sessions cast-iron, black enameled mantel clock, green pillars, gilded decorations & feet, eight-day time & strike, 15 x 10" h. **$165**.

Sessions black-enameled wooden-case mantel clock w/brass feet & applied decorations, eight-day time & strike, 17 x 11" h. **$180**.

Seth Thomas "Arno" adamantine black enameled mantel clock w/gilded & marbleized columns, eight-day time & strike, 12 x 11 1/2" h. **$270**.

Seth Thomas adamantine black enameled mantel clock, w/four columns, gilded decorations & marbleized ends, eight-day time & strike, ca. 1895, 18 x 12" h. **$325**.

Seth Thomas adamantine black enameled mantel clock, four marbleized columns, copper wash finish, eight-day time & strike, 17 1/2 x 12" h. **$300**.

Seth Thomas black enameled adamantine finish
mantel clock, brass dial, feet & lion heads at
each end, dated Sept. 7, 1880, 17 x 11 1/2" h.
$225.

Unknown maker mantel clock w/Grecian figures,
eight-day time & strike, 16 x 12" h. $260.

Waterbury cast-iron black enameled mantel
clock, brass dial, brass applied decorations,
eight-day time & strike, 9 1/2 x 11" h. $275.

E. N. Welch "Albani" marble mantel clock,
porcelain dial, open escapement, beveled
glass, eight-day time & strike (contains the
famous Patti movement), 14 1/2 x 10" h.
$600.

Calendar Clocks

Ansonia "Lily" inkwell calendar clock (left), 30-hour, 7" h. $1,200. Ansonia "Gem" inkwell perpetual calendar clock, 7 1/2" h. $1,400.

Ansonia simple calendar shelf clock, eight-day 8 1/2" h. $350.

L. F. & W. W. Carter rosewood double-dial perpetual calendar, top dial records days & bottom dial records months & dates, eight-day time & strike, 13 1/2 x 21" h. $700.

Close up of calendar dial of **Ingraham** parlor calendar.

Ingraham "Parlor Calendar," w/B. B. Lewis calendar mechanism, ca. 1890, 21 1/2" h. **$600**.

Close up of pendulum behind calendar dial of Ingraham parlor calendar.

Ithaca Calendar Clock Company "Grange" mahogany calendar clock, patented 1866, 12 x 25" h, broken crown lowers value. **$400.**

Ithaca Calendar Clock Company "The Emerald" walnut perpetual calendar shelf clock w/ebony trim. Provisions for the date, day & month are on the lower tablet, eight-day time & strike, 14 1/2 x 33" h. **$3,400.**

Ithaca Calendar Clock Company walnut "Index" w/two patent dates— April 18, 1865 & Aug. 28, 1866, perpetual calendar shelf clock manufactured for Lynch Brothers w/provisions for the date, day & month on the lower round tablet, eight-day time & strike, 17 x 33" h. **$3,500.**

Back of **Ithaca** "No. 3 1/2 Shelf Cottage" calendar clock.

Ithaca Calendar Clock Company "No. 3 1/2 Parlor Calendar" w/walnut-&-ebony trimmed case, ca. 1881, 20 1/2" h. **$1650**.

Ithaca Calendar Clock Company "No. 5" rosewood-case double-dial calendar clock, ca. 1879, 22 1/2" h. **$775**.

Back of **Ithaca** "No. 5" calendar clock

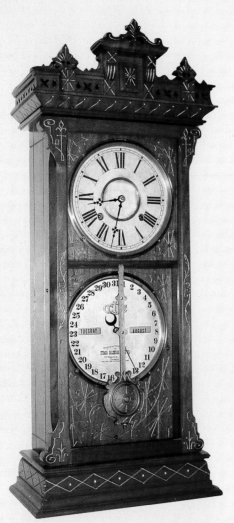

Ithaca Calendar Clock Company "No. 6 1/2 Shelf Belgrade," double-dial eight-day striking calendar clock w/walnut case, ca. 1880, 32" h. $2,400.

Ithaca Calendar Clock Company "No. 7 Shelf Cottage," walnut-case calendar clock, ca. 1874, 22" h. $400.

Close up of Ithaca "No. 7 Shelf Cottage" calendar dial.

Ithaca Calendar Clock Company "No. 8 Shelf Library" walnut perpetual calendar clock, w/burl inlay, 2 x 26 1/2" h. $1,500.

Ithaca Calendar Clock Company "No. 8 Shelf Library" w/walnut case & time & strike movement, ca. 1880, 22 1/2" h. **$350**.

Ithaca Calendar Clock Company "No. 10 Farmer's" calendar shelf clock w/walnut case, ca. 1880, 24" h. **$575**.

Close up of **Ithaca** "No. 10 Farmer's" calendar dial.

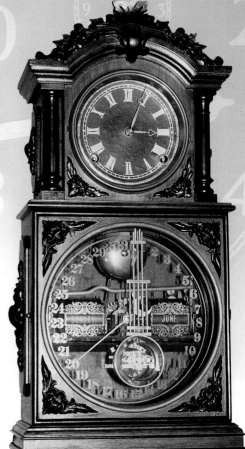

Ithaca Calendar Clock Company walnut perpetual calendar shelf clock w/ebony applied decorations & turned columns. The dates of the month are in gold around the outer rim of the bottom tablet, & the days & months are on rotating tubes behind the tablet, eight-day time & strike, 10 x 20" h. **$4,500.**

Ithaca Calendar Clock Company walnut perpetual calendar shelf clock w/ebony applied decorations & turned columns. The dates are in silver around the outer rim of the bottom tablet, & the two rectangular windows show the day & month, eight-day time & strike, 10 x 28" h. **$3,500.**

Ithaca Calendar Clock Company walnut calendar clock, eight-day time & strike, ca. 1820s, 11 1/2 x 21" h. **$1,795.**

F. Kroeber oak "Summit" centrifugal calendar clock, eight-day time & strike, ca. 1877, 21 1/2" h. **$750**.

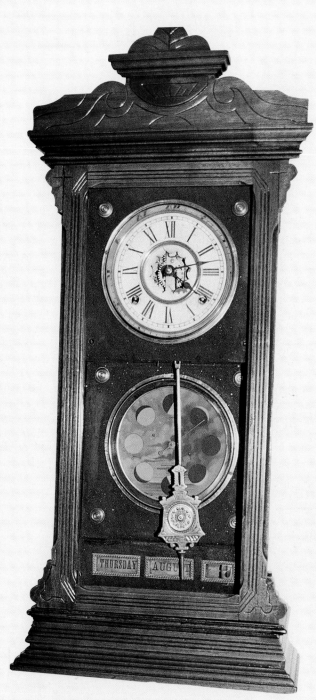

Macomb Calendar Clock Company, walnut perpetual calendar clock, incised carving, moon phases on lower dial, eight-day time & strike, ca. 1882 to 1883, 13 x 28" h. **$5,000**.

Close-up of **F. Kroeber's** "Summit" calendar shelf clock dial, which has dates encircling inner rim & "Calendar Patented July 1877" at the top of the inner circle.

Seth Thomas "Office Calendar No. 2" w/walnut veneer case, ca. 1875, 42 1/2" h. **$1,200.**

The **"Ridgeway"** a 25-year-old walnut reproduction calendar shelf clock, eight-day time & strike, 15 1/2 x 27" h. **$300.**

Close up of **Seth Thomas** "Office Calendar No. 2" calendar dial.

New Haven oak perpetual calendar shelf clock, w/two parallel dials, inscribed lines, eight-day time only, 14 x 13" h. **$2,800.**

Seth Thomas eight-day, two-weight, double-dial parlor calendar clock w/rosewood case, ca. 1865, 30 1/2" h. **$1,200**.

Seth Thomas oak kitchen calendar clock w/applied & incised decorations, eight-day time & strike, 15 x 23" h. **$295**.

Seth Thomas rosewood double-dial calendar clock, eight-day time & strike, 14 x 26" h. **$1,495**.

Southern Calendar Clock Company mahogany "Fashion Number 2," calendar clock, eight-day time & strike, Pat. July 4, 1876. The cases & time movements were made by Seth Thomas & the calendar mechanism used the Andrews Calendar patent. The company was located in St. Louis, Missouri. **$1,750**.

Unknown maker, mahogany simple calendar shelf clock, time only, eight-day, pendulum movement, 10 x 17" h. **$750**.

Carriage Clocks

Boston Clock Company carriage clock, brass frame & carrying handle, 3 1/2 x 5" h. **$350-$450**.

Boston Clock Company carriage clock, patented Dec. 20, 1880, brass case, porcelain dial, tandem wind spring movement, 30-hour, time only, 4 x 6 1/2" h. **$3,750**.

F. Kroeber carriage clock, brass case, glass sides & time only, ca. 1889, 8" h. **$200**.

Seth Thomas "Legacy" model
mahogany carriage shelf clock, eight-day
time & strike w/Westminster chimes, ca.
1951, 10 3/4 x 14" h. **$150**.

Plato brass digital carriage clock,
patented July 7, 1903, 3 x 6" h. **$500**.

Waterbury repeater carriage
clock, brass frame & carrying
handle, 3 1/2 x 4" h. **$350-$450**.

Waterbury brass carriage clock
w/jeweled movement, patented June 4,
1907, 3 x 4 1/2" h. **$460**.

Gothic Clocks

Ansonia mahogany ribbon-stripe Gothic shelf clock, eight-day time & strike, strikes hours & half hours, 8 x 12" h. **$185**.

M. W. Atkins & Company eight-day steeple clock w/rosewood-veneered front, mahogany-veneered sides, & William B. Fenn faux acid-etch-style glass, ca. 1848, 19 3/4" h. **$460**.

J. J. Beals & Company 30-hour rosewood-front steeple w/alarm, solid escape wheel, & William B. Fenn faux acid-etch-style heart & lyre glass, ca. 1850, 19 1/2" h. **$140**.

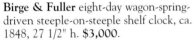

Birge & Fuller eight-day wagon-spring-driven steeple-on-steeple shelf clock, ca. 1848, 27 1/2" h. **$3,000**.

Brewster & Ingrahams eight-day onion-top Gothic shelf clock, ca. 1850, 20 1/2" h. **$1,500**.

Brewster & Ingrahams, Kirk's patent beehive shelf clock w/eight-day rack-&-snail strike movement & rosewood case, ca. 1845, 19" h. **$500**.

Brewster & Ingrahams, Kirk's patent iron-backplate beehive shelf clock w/mahogany case & eight-day rack-&-snail strike movement, ca. 1844, 19" h. **$900**.

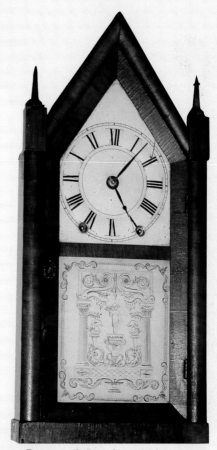

Brewster & Ingrahams 30-hour time & strike steeple clock w/rosewood-veneer case. Rare early model that is a little narrower than later models, ca. 1848, 19" h. **$200**.

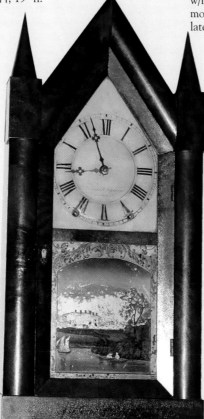

Brewster & Ingrahams 30-hour time & strike iron-backplate steeple clock, w/mahogany veneer, ca. 1845, 20" h. **$200**.

Brewster & Ingrahams eight-day time & strike double-steeple shelf clock, ca. 1850, 19 1/4" h. **$675**.

Brewster & Ingrahams, Kirk's patent iron-backplate steeple clock w/eight-day time & strike & rosewood veneer case, first model w/full iron backplate & rack-&-snail strike, ca. 1845, 19 3/4" h. **$800**.

Brewster & Ingrahams mahogany ribbed Gothic shelf clock, original brass springs replaced, eight-day time & strike, 10 1/2 x 19" h. **$450**.

Brewster & Ingrahams burled walnut Gothic shelf clock, brass springs, replaced tablet & hands, eight-day time & strike, 10 1/2 x 19" h. **$400**.

E. C. Brewster & Son 30-hour time, strike & alarm steeple clock, ca. 1855, 19 1/2" h. **$400**.

J. C. Brown eight-day time & strike steeple clock w/rosewood-case, ca. 1855, 19 3/4" h. **$275**.

J. C. Brown rosewood ribbed front Gothic shelf clock, time & strike, ca. 1855, 10 1/2 x 19" h. **$1,400**.

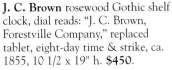

J. C. Brown rosewood Gothic shelf clock, dial reads: "J. C. Brown, Forestville Company," replaced tablet, eight-day time & strike, ca. 1855, 10 1/2 x 19" h. **$450**.

J. C. Brown rosewood steeple clock, time & strike, ca. 1850, 10 x 19 1/2" h. **$400**.

J. C. Brown & Company rosewood ripple front steeple shelf clock, ca. 1855, time & strike, 10 x 20" h. **$1,750**.

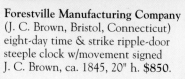

Forestville Manufacturing Company
(J. C. Brown, Bristol, Connecticut)
eight-day time & strike ripple-door
steeple clock w/movement signed
J. C. Brown, ca. 1845, 20" h. **$850.**

W. L. Gilbert rosewood
steeple clock, 30-hour,
time & strike, spring
driven, 11 x 20" h.
$150.

Ingraham mahogany-stained
beehive clock, eight-day time
& strike, 9 x 13 1/2" h. **$190.**

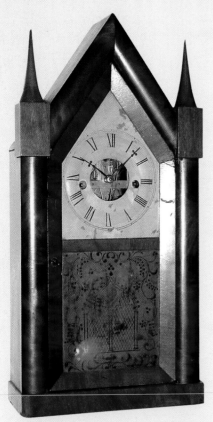

Chauncey Jerome 30-hour striking steeple clock w/mahogany-veneered case, ca. 1848, 19 3/4" h. **$175**.

Elisha Manross 30-hour time & strike steeple clock w/mahogany-veneer case, ca. 1850, 19 3/4" h. **$425**.

Jerome & Co. walnut-stained Gothic shelf clock, patented Oct. 18, 1870, eight-day time & strike, 11 x 16 1/2" h. **$250**.

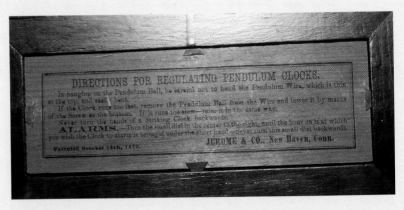

Directions for regulating pendulum clocks, found inside the **Jerome & Co.** Gothic shelf clock.

New Haven 30-hour time, strike & alarm miniature steeple clock w/rosewood-veneered case, ca. 1870, 14 3/4" h. **$150**.

Seth Thomas "Prospect Number 1" mahogany Gothic shelf clock, time & strike, ca. 1910, 13 1/2" h. **$220**.

Pond & Barnes eight-day time & strike beehive shelf clock w/rosewood case. The dial has been nicely repainted but has a spurious signature of J. C. Brown. The original movement is marked "Forestville," & came from the Brown shop, but Brown would have shipped a resale clock w/unsigned dial, ca. 1850, 19" h. **$275**.

Seth Thomas walnut sharp-Gothic steeple clock, eight-day time & strike, ca. 1902, 11 x 19" h. **$300**.

Smith & Goodrich 30-hour time & strike steeple clock w/mahogany veneer case, ca. 1848, 19 3/4" h. **$275**.

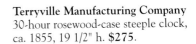

Terryville Manufacturing Company 30-hour rosewood-case steeple clock, ca. 1855, 19 1/2" h. **$275**.

Tiffany battery-operated mahogany
Gothic shelf clock, beveled glass,
time only, ca. 1895, 10 x 16" h.
$1,250.

Waterbury rosewood Gothic steeple,
shelf clock, 30-hour, time & strike,
ca. 1870, 19 1/2" h. **$225**.

Waterbury mahogany Gothic shelf
clock w/visible escapement. eight-
day time & strike, 9 x 12 1/2" h.
$275.

Waterbury eight-day steeple clock w/mahogany-veneer case, ca. 1870, 18 1/2" h. **$175**.

Waterbury miniature 30-hour steeple clock w/alarm & rosewood-veneer front & door & mahogany-veneer side, ca. 1875, 15 1/4" h. **$75**.

Waterbury, for Juan Shaw, Buenos Ayres, 30-hour time, strike & alarm, ca. 1880, 19" h. **$100**.

E. N. Welch Manufacturing Company
30-hour time, strike & alarm steeple
clock w/mahogany, ca. 1865, 19 1/2" h.
$170.

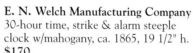

**E. N. Welch
Manufacturing Company**
30-hour rosewood minia-
ture-steeple clock, ca.
1870, 14 1/2" h. **$100**.

**E. N. Welch
Manufacturing Company**
mahogany steeple shelf
clock, time, strike, &
alarm, 10 x 19 1/2" h.
$300.

Mantel Clocks

Ansonia "Cygnet" metal mantel clock, w/cherub on top holding a wreath, Syrian bronze finish, porcelain dial, eight-day time & strike, ca. 1906, 7 1/2 x 12 3/4" h. **$600**.

Ansonia "Lydia" cast-iron mantel clock, open escapement, w/cherubs on top of clock, eight-day time & strike, w/matching pair of urns, 19 1/2" h. **$3,000**.

Ansonia "Minerva" metal mantel clock, w/seated lady on top, gilded case, porcelain dial, open escapement, time & strike, ca. 1894, 11 x 16 1/2" h. **$500**.

Ansonia "The Virginia" cast-iron mantel clock w/statue, "Opera" on top of clock, open escapement, brass & silver dial, silver panels on each side of clock, eight-day time & strike, w/matching pair of urns, 21 x 25" h. **$4,500**.

Two reproduction metal figures used as clock tops, 7" h. **$15 each**.

Cast metal ornament for use on flat top clock. Many similar ornaments were available from Ansonia Clock Company, 9 x 6" h. **$75.**

Ansonia metal mantel clock w/white marbleized case, gilt decorations & copper face, eight-day time & strike, 11 x 18 1/2" h. **$500.**

Ansonia metal mantel clock w/Syrian bronze finish, porcelain dial, open escapement, eight-day time & strike, 11 x 17 1/2" h. **$700**.

W. M. Gilbert wooden mantel clock w/bell, eight-day time & strike, early 1900s, 17 x 19" h. **$695**.

W. L. Gilbert oak tambour mantel clock, time & strike, ca. 1880, 9 1/2" h. **$110**.

E. Ingraham miniature (baby camelback) wooden tambour mantel clock, metal dial, 8 1/2 x 5 1/2" h. **$85**.

E. Ingraham oak mantel clock, time & strike, ca. 1895, 10" h. **$120**.

Ingraham marbleized wooden mantel clock w/brass feet, eight-day time & strike, 14 x 12" h. **$105**.

Ingraham mahogany tambour mantel clock, eight-day time & strike, ca. mid 1900s, 19 1/2 x 10" h. **$155**.

New Haven mantel clock w/marbleized finish & applied brass decorations, eight-day time & strike, 15 x 10" h. **$265**.

The Plymouth Clock Company wooden tambour mantel clock, eight-day time & strike, 19 x 9 1/2" h. **$125**.

W. F. Rogers Manufacturing Co. (Chicago, Illinois) miniature tambour clock, 3 1/2 x 7 1/4", 3 1/2" h. **$95.**

Sessions Clock Co. "Dulciana" mahogany tambour mantel clock, eight-day time & strike, 21 1/2 x 10" h. **$175.**

Sessions Clock Co. mahogany tambour mantel clock, eight-day time & strike. Westminster chimes, patented 1929, 18 x 17 1/2" h. **$175.**

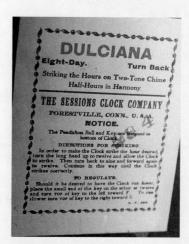

Label on the back of the **Sessions** "Dulciana" mantel clock.

Sessions Clock Co. cherry stained mantel clock, six columns, gilded feet & lion heads, eight-day time & strike, ca. 1910, 14 1/2 x 10 1/2" h. **$175**.

Sessions Clock Co. mahogany-case camelback mantel clock, eight-day time & strike, 17 x 11" h. **$285**.

Sessions Clock Co. small wooden-case mantel clock w/gilded pillars, 30-hour, 7 1/2 x 8 1/2" h. **$200**.

Sessions Clock Co. mahogany shelf clock, eight-day time & strike, early 1900s, 17 x 11" h. **$240**.

Seth Thomas "Domino" walnut shelf clock, eight-day time & strike, 8 x 9 1/2" h. **$275**.

Seth Thomas adamantine-finished mantel clock, eight-day time & strike, early 1900s, **$280**.

Seth Thomas mantel clock, black adamantine-finished case w/six decorative pillars & brass decorations, eight-day time & strike, early 1900s, 18 x 11" h. **$200**.

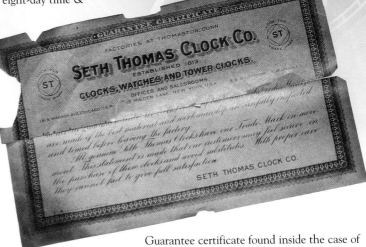

Guarantee certificate found inside the case of the **Seth Thomas** mantel clock.

Seth Thomas adamantine mottled marbleized finish mantel clock, eight-day time & strike, 17 x 12" h. **$300**.

Seth Thomas adamantine (rosewood finish) tambour mantel clock, eight-day time & strike, 17 1/2 x 10 1/2" h. **$245**.

Seth Thomas wooden case tambour mantel clock, 6 1/2 x 3 1/2" h. **$85**.

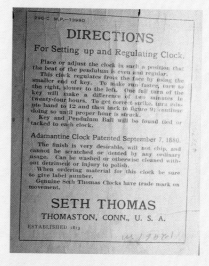

Seth Thomas adamantine (mahogany finish) mantel clock, eight-day time & strike, 9 x 9 1/2" h. **$295**.

Label on the back of **Seth Thomas** tambour mantel clock.

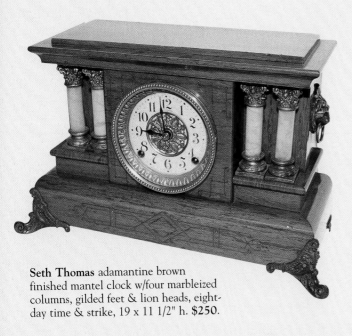

Seth Thomas adamantine brown finished mantel clock w/four marbleized columns, gilded feet & lion heads, eight-day time & strike, 19 x 11 1/2" h. **$250**.

Seth Thomas adamantine ivory finished mantel clock w/six columns, gilded feet & lion heads, eight-day time & strike, 17 1/2 x 11 1/2" h. **$300**.

Seth Thomas adamantine mottled gold finish mantel clock, brass dial, eight-day time & strike, 17 x 12" h. **$300**. A label on back states that this clock was made especially for a company in Rockford, Illinois.

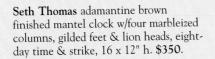

Seth Thomas adamantine brown finished mantel clock w/four marbleized columns, gilded feet & lion heads, eight-day time & strike, 16 x 12" h. **$350**.

Tiffany & Co., New York, marble-base shelf clock w/bell, eight-day time & strike, 11 x 20", 18" h. **$3,500**.

Unknown maker, miniature metal mantel clock, corner columns, time only, 4 1/2 x 4" h. **$115**.

Unknown maker bim bam (double chimer) tambour clock, eight-day time only. **$195**.

Waterbury mantel clock, eight-day time & strike, 10 1/2 x 10 1/2" h. **$195**.

Waterbury mahogany-stained mantel clock, eight-day time & strike, ca. 1920, 13 x 12" h. **$195**.

Waterbury bim-bam (double chimer) tambour clock, strikes both hour & half-hour, 22 x 10 1/2" h. **$155**.

Waterbury mahogany finished mantel clock, imitation mercury pendulum, glass door w/brass frame, eight-day time & strike, 6 1/2 x 9 1/2" h. **$275**.

Metal and Iron-Front Clocks

American Clock Company 30-hour bronze-finish iron-front shelf clock, ca. 1855, 12" h. **$250**.

American Clock Company metal case shelf clock, multi-colored w/birds & flowers on case, 30-hour, time & strike, spring driven, 13 x 16" h. **$400**.

American Clock Company (address on label is #3 Cortlandt, New Broadway) metal mantel clock w/mother-of-pearl inlay, brass dial, eight-day time & strike (winders below dial), 8 1/2 x 16" h. **$250**.

Brass vanity shelf clock, 3 1/2 x 5" h. **$75**.

Ansonia iron shelf clock w/brass & gild coating & 4" d. porcelain face, eight-day time & strike, 4 1/2 x 8", 13 1/2" h. **$895**.

New Haven "Acme" brass clock w/top handle, 30-hour, time only **$350**.

New Haven metal-frame shelf clock, 30-hour, ca. 1890, 8 1/2" x 12" h. **$500**.

New Haven iron shelf clock w/gild finish, eight-day time & strike, made in 1905, 10 1/2 x 12" h. **$685**.

New Haven gilded cast-iron vanity clock, 2 1/2" d. dial, 6" h. **$115**.

New Haven metal front shelf clock w/cupid figure, 4 1/2 x 7" h. **$145**.

Parker Clock Company brass mantel clock w/two cupids holding up the lamp posts, which have jeweled inserts, 30-hour, time only, 7 x 6 1/2" h. **$1,200.**

Parker Clock Company iron front shelf clock w/visible escapement (on top of clock), 30-hour, time only, 6" h. **$1,000.** Right, iron front shelf clock w/visible escapement (on bottom of clock), 30-hour, time only, 6" h. **$1,000.**

Parker Clock Company metal front mantel clocks, cupids carrying clocks, gilded cast-iron cases, 30-hour, time only, Left clock, 6 1/2" h. **$450.** Right clock, 5 1/2" h. **$400.**

Semca brass vanity shelf clock, mid 1900s,
4 1/2 x 6" h. **$65**.

Unmarked metal front mantel clock w/four frogs,
one singing, two playing instruments & one sitting
at the base of cast-iron case, 30-hour, time only,
9 1/2 x 12" h. **$250**.

Seth Thomas metal front mantel clock,
nickel-plated over brass, minute hand, time &
alarm, 7 x 9" h. **$150**.

Unmarked metal front mantel clock, patented Feb. 6, 1904, brass finish, time only, 7 1/2 x 11" h. **$135.**

Unmarked metal front mantel clock, porcelain & brass dial, gilded case, 30-hour, time only, 3 x 4" h. **$150.**

Waterbury "Hornet" brass clock w/ivory dial, glass cylinder, 30-hour, time only, ca. 1900, 2 3/4" d. **$225.**

Waterbury bronzed-finish iron shelf clock w/alarm, late 1800s or early 1900s, 11 x 13 1/2" h. **$595.**

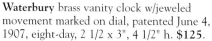

Waterbury brass vanity clock w/jeweled movement marked on dial, patented June 4, 1907, eight-day, 2 1/2 x 3", 4 1/2" h. **$125**.

E. N. Welch gilded metal shelf clock, eight-day time & strike, ca. 1880, 11 3/4 x 13" h. **$350**.

Western Clock Manufacturing Company, La Salle, Illinois, brass finished iron-front shelf clock w/female figure holding up the clock, 30-hour, time only, 6 1/2 x 12" h. **$200**.

Oak Clocks

Ansonia "Dalton" oak shelf clock, incised designs, eight-day time & strike, ca. 1885, 12 x 23" h. **$275**.

Ansonia "Triumph" oak shelf clock, mirror sides w/brass cupid statues & other applied brass decorations, eight-day time & strike, ca. 1890, 17 x 24 1/2" h. **$750**.

Ansonia "Trivoli" oak shelf clock, pressed & applied decorations, brass dial, patented June 18, 1882, eight-day time & strike, 11 1/2 x 15" h. **$300**.

Ansonia oak kitchen clock w/pressed designs, eight-day time & strike w/alarm, ca. early 1900s, 14 1/2 x 23" h. **$240**.

Ansonia oak shelf clock, brass dial, incised & applied decorations, eight-day time & strike, 12 1/2 x 17" h. **$300**.

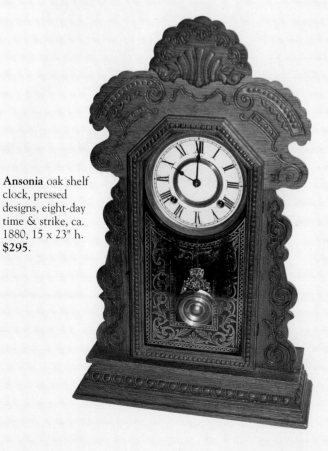

Ansonia oak shelf clock, pressed designs, eight-day time & strike, ca. 1880, 15 x 23" h. **$295**.

Ansonia oak kitchen clock w/applied & incised decorations, eight-day time & strike, 14 1/2 x 23" h. **$265**.

W. L. Gilbert "Concord" oak kitchen clock w/steam-pressed designs on case, eight-day time & strike, ca. 1910 to 1920, 14 x 24" h. **$300**.

W. L. Gilbert "Egypt" oak shelf clock (part of the Egyptian series), pressed designs, eight-day time & strike, 17 x 25" h. **$300**.

Label inside "Egyptian No. 1" clock.

W. L. Gilbert "Egyptian No. 1" oak kitchen clock w/alarm, eight-day time & strike, 17 x 24 1/2" h. **$695**.

W. L. Gilbert "Nebo" oak shelf clock, incised designs, eight-day time, strike, & alarm, 11 1/2 x 22" h. **$500**.

W. L. Gilbert "Mogul" oak shelf clock (part of the Egyptian series), pressed design, eight-day time, strike, & alarms, ca. 1895, 16 x 24" h. **$300**.

W. L. Gilbert "Pasha" oak shelf clock (part of the Egyptian series), pressed designs, eight-day time, strike, & alarm, ca. 1905, 15 1/2 x 25" h. **$300**.

W. L. Gilbert "Pyramid" oak shelf clock (part of the Egyptian series), pressed designs, eight-day time & strike, 15 1/2 x 24" h. **$300**.

W. M. Gilbert oak kitchen clock w/pressed designs, eight-day time & strike w/alarm, 14 1/2 x 23" h. **$325**.

W. L. Gilbert oak shelf clock, incised carving, eight-day time & strike, ca. 1890, 14 x 22" h. **$275**.

W. L. Gilbert oak shelf clock, pressed designs, eight-day time & strike, ca. 1901, 15 1/2 x 23" h. **$245**.

E. Ingraham "Post" oak shelf clock, incised designs & applied decorations, eight-day time & strike, ca. 1910, 15 x 23" h. **$275**.

E. Ingraham "Jasper" oak shelf clock, basket weave pressed designs & applied decorations, eight-day time & strike, ca. 1905, 15 x 23" h. **$300**.

E. Ingraham oak shelf clock, pressed designs, eight-day time, strike, & alarm, 15 x 22" h. **$225**.

Lux oak shelf clock, octagon face, brass dial, 8 x 7 1/2" h. **$95**.

Ingraham oak kitchen clock w/pressed designs, eight-day time & strike, 14 1/2 x 22" h. **$260**.

New Haven oak shelf clock w/side mirrors, pressed designs, eight-day time, strike, & alarm, 16 x 24" h. **$450**.

Sessions oak shelf clock, Mission-style w/brass Arabic numerals, eight-day time only, ca. 1910, 8 x 14 1/2" h. **$175**.

Sessions oak shelf clock, pressed designs, eight-day time & strike, ca. 1880, 15 x 23" h. **$300**.

Seth Thomas "New York" oak shelf clock (part of the College series), incised carving & applied decorations, eight-day time, strike, & alarm, 14 x 23" h. **$300**.

Seth Thomas "Cambridge" oak shelf clock (part of the College series), incised carving & applied decorations, eight-day time, strike, & alarm 14 x 22 1/2" h. **$250**.

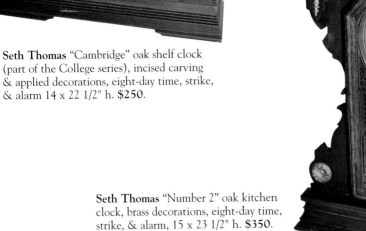

Seth Thomas "Number 2" oak kitchen clock, brass decorations, eight-day time, strike, & alarm, 15 x 23 1/2" h. **$350**.

Seth Thomas "Yale" oak shelf clock, (part of the College series), incised carving & applied decorations, eight-day time, strike, & alarm, 15 x 23" h. $250.

Seth Thomas oak shelf clock, applied metal decorations, eight-day time, strike, & alarm, 15 x 22 1/2" h. $275.

Seth Thomas oak shelf clock, applied metal decorations, eight-day time, strike, & alarm, 15 x 23" h. $275.

Seth Thomas oak shelf clock, applied metal decorations, eight-day time, strike, & alarm, 14 1/2 x 23" h. **$275**.

Seth Thomas oak parlor clock, eight-day time & strike, ca. 1890, 15 x 23" h. **$200**.

Waterbury "Felix" oak shelf clock, incised carving, eight-day time, strike, & alarm, ca. 1910, 15 x 22" h. **$300**.

Waterbury "Mansfield" oak shelf clock, incised carving & applied decorations, ca. 1890, 15 x 21 1/2" h. **$250**.

Waterbury oak shelf clock, applied copper decorations, including moose head near top, eight-day time & strike, ca. 1899, 15 x 22" h. **$265**.

Waterbury oak shelf clock, incised carving & applied decorations, simple calendar attachment, eight-day time & strike, 15 x 22" h. **$550**.

Parlor Clocks

Ansonia "Dispatch" parlor clock w/ original ebony finish, 13 1/2 x 31" h. **$700**.

Ansonia "Harwich" cherry shelf clock, open escapement, ceramic dial, time & strike, ca. 1895, 12" h. **$225**.

Ansonia "The Herald" enameled wooden case, time & strike, 9 1/2" w. 16" h. **$250**.

Ansonia "Mobile" walnut parlor shelf clock, glass sides, incised carving, eight-day time & strike, ca. 1910, 20" h. **$525**.

Ansonia walnut parlor clock w/brass decorations, eight-day time & strike, 16 x 24 1/2" h. **$675**.

Ansonia "Triumph" walnut parlor clock w/ mirrored sides, eight-day time & strike, 17 x 24" h. **$600**.

Ansonia rosewood Gothic shelf clock, offset pendulum, time only, ca. 1878, 10" h. **$135**.

Benedict Mfg. Co. mahogany shelf clock, medallion below dial, time only, 3 1/2 x 4" h. **$75**.

Ansonia black case shelf clock, 30-hour, alarm, 7 1/2 x 10 1/2" h. **$100**. Right, white shelf clock, 30-hour, time & alarm, 7 1/2 x 10 1/2" h. **$110**.

W. L. Gilbert rosewood cottage shelf clock w/octagon top, at Winsted Connecticut, eight-day time & strike, ca. 1878-1885, 10 x 13 1/2" h. **$175**.

W. L. Gilbert "Amphion" walnut parlor shelf clock, etched beveled mirrors, mirror pendulum, applied decorations, Lincoln drape silk screening on door, 16 1/2 x 25" h. **$2,000**.

W. L. Gilbert "Attal" walnut parlor shelf clock, incised carvings, eight-day time, strike, & alarm, 20 1/2" h. **$350**.

W. L. Gilbert "Eastlake" walnut parlor shelf clock, incised carving & applied decorations, eight-day time & strike, 22" h. **$500**.

W. L. Gilbert "Mitra" walnut parlor shelf clock, incised carving, side columns, eight-day time & strike, 12 x 22" h. **$350**.

W. L. Gilbert rosewood shelf clock, spring driven, ca. 1860, 13 x 19 1/2" h. **$250**.

E. Ingraham walnut parlor shelf clock, incised carving & applied decorations, sharp Gothic style, eight-day time, strike, & alarm, 22" h. **$275**.

E. Ingraham walnut parlor shelf clock, applied decorations, ionic style, eight-day time & strike, ca. 1895, 22" h. **$400**.

E. Ingraham walnut parlor shelf clock, incised carving, eight-day time, strike, & alarm, 15 x 21" ca. 1890, h. **$225**.

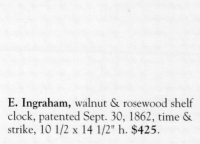

E. Ingraham, walnut & rosewood shelf clock, patented Sept. 30, 1862, time & strike, 10 1/2 x 14 1/2" h. **$425**.

Jerome & Co., New Haven, Connecticut, walnut shelf clock, ebony trim, 30-hour, time & strike, ca. 1855, 11 1/2 x 16 1/2" h. **$225**.

F. Kroeber "Dictator" rosewood parlor shelf clock, 30-hour, time & strike, ca. 1882, 17" h. **$175**.

F. Kroeber "Chalet" walnut parlor shelf clock, pendulum cover removed to expose pendulum, eight-day time & strike, ca. 1887, 17 1/2" h. **$265**.

F. Kroeber "Galena" walnut parlor shelf clock, incised carving, applied burl decorations, pewter trim, eight-day time & strike, ca. 1874, 23" h. **$440**.

F. Kroeber "Fearless" walnut parlor shelf clock, incised carving, 30-hour, time & strike, ca. 1887, 18" h. **$250**.

F. Kroeber "Kansas" walnut parlor shelf clock, carved drop & upright finials, eight-day time & strike, ca. 1881, 20" h. **$450**.

F. Kroeber, "Library" walnut parlor shelf clock, burled walnut, applied decorations, indicator pendulum, eight-day time & strike, 18 x 24" h. **$1,800.**

F. Kroeber "Langtry" walnut parlor shelf clock, incised carving, side pillars & top finials, eight-day time & strike, 9 x 23" h. **$2,200.**

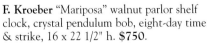

F. Kroeber "Mariposa" walnut parlor shelf clock, crystal pendulum bob, eight-day time & strike, 16 x 22 1/2" h. **$750.**

F. Kroeber "Occidental" walnut parlor shelf clock, mirror sides w/brass statues, applied brass decorations, incised carving, turned side columns, cut glass star bob, eight-day time & strike, ca. 1887, 25" h. **$800**.

F. Kroeber "Rambler" walnut parlor shelf clock, incised carving, Jacob's patent "Slow and fast" on pendulum, eight-day time & strike, ca. 1890, 11 x 20" h. **$325**.

F. Kroeber walnut parlor shelf clock, incised carving & applied decorations, eight-day time & strike, ca. 1882, 21" h. **$225**.

New Haven "Tuscan" rosewood shelf clock, eight-day time & strike, 10 1/2 x 17 1/2" h. **$475**.

New Haven walnut shelf clock, incised lines & applied decorations, eight-day time & strike, 14 x 21 1/2" h. **$225**.

New Haven walnut parlor clock, eight-day time & strike, 13 x 20" h., dial missing. **$225**.

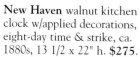

New Haven walnut kitchen clock w/applied decorations, eight-day time & strike, ca. 1880s, 13 1/2 x 22" h. **$275**.

Pomeroy walnut shelf clock, eight-day time & strike, ca. 1820s, 4 1/4" d., 11 1/2 x 16" h. **$250**.

Roswell-Kimberly rosewood shelf clock, w/top finials & columns, eight-day time & strike, ca. 1850 to 1860, 11 x 21" h. **$500**.

Seth Thomas "Albany" walnut parlor shelf clock, applied decorations, eight-day time, strike, & alarm, 11 x 20 1/2" h. **$325**.

Russell and Jones walnut parlor clock, incised carving, eight-day time, strike, & alarm, 14 x 22 1/2" h. **$375**.

Seth Thomas "Atlanta" parlor shelf clock, side pillars w/gilt trim, eight-day time & strike, 12 1/2 x 20" h. **$275**.

Seth Thomas "Norfolk" walnut parlor shelf clock, incised carving, eight-day time, strike, & alarm, ca. 1890, 12 x 19 1/2" h. **$325**.

Seth Thomas "Tacoma" walnut parlor shelf clock, incised carving, winders under dial, eight-day time & strike, ca. 1870, 23" h. **$350**.

Seth Thomas walnut Eastlake-style parlor clock w/incised decorations, eight-day time & strike, 11 x 18 1/2" h. **$280**.

Seth Thomas mahogany
cottage clock w/gilded pillars,
30-hour time & strike,
ca. 1830s, 10 1/2 x 16" h. **$295**.

Seth Thomas mahogany shelf clock,
eight-day time & strike, late 1800s,
$200.

Seth Thomas mahogany shelf clock
w/game birds on tablet, eight-day time
& strike, late 1800s, 12 x 18" h. **$395**.

Seth Thomas stained parlor shelf clock, incised carving & railing on top, eight-day time, strike, & alarm, ca. 1890, 13 x 21" h. **$450**.

Seth Thomas mahogany flat top shelf clock, Geneva stops to prevent over-winding, eight-day time & strike, ca. 1866-1870 (Plymouth Hollow label), 11 1/2 x 15 1/2" h. **$200**.

Seth Thomas mahogany cottage shelf clock, 30-hour time & strike, strikes hours only, ca. 1865, 10 x 13 3/4" h. **$180**.

Unknown maker walnut parlor clock, Eastlake-style, 13 x 22" h. **$395**.

Waterbury "Melrose" walnut parlor clock, incised carving, movement is stamped w/Waterbury patent, Sept. 22, 1874, eight-day time & strike, ca. 1881, 12 1/2 x 21" h. **$275**.

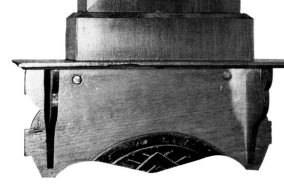

Waterbury "Cottage No. 1" mahogany shelf clock, 30-hour, time & strike, 8 x 11 3/4" h. **$225**.

Waterbury walnut parlor clock, Eastlake-style w/applied decorations, eight-day time & strike, 12 x 21" h. **$250**.

Waterbury mahogany shelf clock, 30-hour, time only, ca. 1870 to 1880, 8 x 11 1/4" h. **$165**.

Waterbury walnut parlor shelf clock, incised carving, Sandwich glass pendulum, 30-hour, time & strike, 12 x 18 1/2" h. **$200**.

E. N. Welch, "The Boss" walnut parlor shelf clock, incised carving, ca. 1881, 12 1/2 x 20" h. **$175**.

E. N. Welch "Dolaro" walnut parlor shelf clock, incised carving, eight-day time, strike, & alarm, ca. 1885, 14 x 22 1/2" h. **$350**.

E. N. Welch "Dandelion" walnut parlor shelf clock, incised carving, eight-day time, strike, & alarm, 10 x 17 1/2" h. **$200**.

E. N. Welch "Eclipse" walnut parlor shelf clock, incised carving, eight-day time, strike, & alarm. Originally this clock was a wall hanger, but it was so successful it was changed to a shelf clock. For a while it was a premium for Metropolitan Mfg., New York, 15 1/2 x 24" h. **$450**.

E. N. Welch "Empress" rosewood shelf clock, eight-day time & strike, ca. 1875, 10 1/2 x 16" h. **$250**.

E. N. Welch "Empress VP" mahogany shelf clock, simulated mercury pendulum, eight-day time & strike, 11 1/2 x 17 3/4" h. **$275**.

E. N. Welch "Handel" walnut parlor shelf clock, incised carving, applied decorations, "ENW" embossed on pendulum, eight-day time & strike, 14 x 23" h. **$300**.

E. N. Welch "Litta" walnut parlor shelf clock, incised carving, glass center pendulum, eight-day time & strike, 16 x 23 1/2" h. **$350**.

E. N. Welch "Pepite" walnut parlor shelf clock, incised carving, Sandwich glass pendulum & applied decorations, eight-day time & strike, ca. 1887, 14 x 23" h. **$350**.

E. N. Welch "Nanon" walnut parlor shelf clock, incised carving, Sandwich glass pendulum, eight-day time & strike, ca. 1890, 15 1/2 x 22" h. **$400**.

E. N. Welch "Roze" walnut parlor shelf clock, incised carving & applied decorations, eight-day time & strike, 13 1/2 x 21" h. **$325**.

E. N. Welch "Scachi" walnut parlor clock (named after Italian operatic soprano), incised carving, finials, Patti movement, eight-day time & strike, 1884-1893, 12 x 19 3/4" h. **$1,100**.

E. N. Welch "Titiens" walnut parlor shelf clock (named after German soprano, Theresa Titiens), finials, decorative turnings on stiles, porcelain dial, B. B. Lewis 30-day movement, time only, 1877-1884, 16 x 23 1/2" h. **$2,500**.

E. N. Welch "Tycon" walnut parlor shelf clock, incised carving, Sandwich glass pendulum, eight-day time & strike, 14 x 23" h. **$400**.

E. N. Welch "The Tulip" walnut parlor shelf clock, incised carving, 13 x 19 1/2" h. **$250**.

E. N. Welch "Weber" parlor clock, eight-day time & strike, ca. 1890, 14 x 21" h. **$300**.

E. N. Welch "Weber" walnut parlor shelf clock, incised carving, applied decorations, eight-day time, strike, & alarm, 14 x 21" h. **$300**.

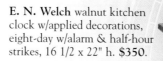

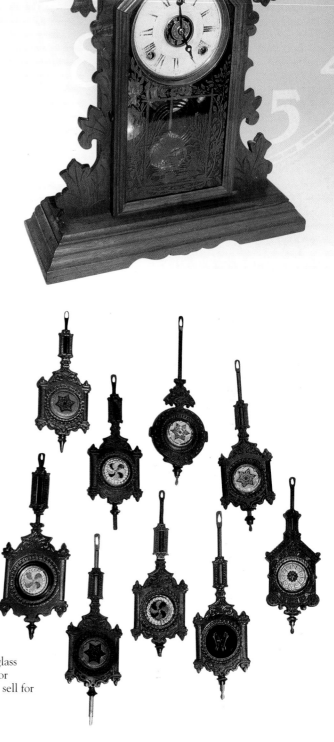

E. N. Welch walnut kitchen clock w/applied decorations, eight-day w/alarm & half-hour strikes, 16 1/2 x 22" h. $350.

E. N. Welch rosewood shelf clock, applied decorations, time & strike, & alarm, ca. 1875, 12 x 19" h. $375.

Welch reproduction Sandwich glass pendulums. Reproductions sell for around $20; original pendulums sell for $80-$145.

Welch, Spring & Co. "Cary" rosewood parlor clock, (named after American contralto Annie Louise Cary), four decoratively turned columns, Patti movement, eight-day time & strike, 12 1/4 x 20 1/2" h. **$1,400**.

Welch, Spring & Co. "Hauck" walnut parlor shelf clock, incised carving, eight-day time & strike, 14 x 22 1/2" h. **$350**.

Welch, Spring & Co. "Gerster" walnut parlor clock (named after Hungarian soprano Etelka Gerster), four decoratively turned columns, Patti movement, eight-day time & strike, 12 1/2 x 18 1/2" h. **$1,400**.

Welch, Spring & Co. "The Patti" rosewood parlor shelf clock (named after Spanish operatic prima donna, Adelina Patti), four decoratively turned columns, glass sides, half-hour strike, eight-day time & strike, 12 1/4 x 18 3/4" h. **$1,400.**

Welch, Spring & Co. stained parlor shelf clock, incised carving, pendulum reads "E. N. W.," eight-day time & strike, 12 1/2 x 21" h. **$300.**

Welch, Spring & Co. "Patti N. 2 VP" or "The Baby Patti" rosewood parlor shelf clock, four decoratively turned pillars, eight-day time only, double spring, ca. 1889, 7 1/2 x 10 1/2" h. **$3,800.**

Chapter 8
Novelty Clocks

To be classified as a novelty, a clock must have a unique function in sounding or telling time, as well as a specialized configuration. When the New Haven Clock Company developed "The Best Show Window Attraction Ever Made," it was called the "Flying Pendulum" or "Ignatz" clock. This one-day, time-only clock was patented October 9, 1882. People enjoyed watching it in action as the pendulum, a ball on a string, swung from side to side and wound and unwound on outer posts.

Two-timer is the name given to a clock that has a dual function. One example is the combination of cigar cutter and clock. Another is an illuminated alarm clock lit by a match when the alarm rings. Examples of these novelties are illustrated in this chapter.

"Sambo," "Topsy," and "Continental" were three novelty clocks produced between 1874 and 1912 that featured eye movements. As the pendulum swung, the eyes moved up and down. Bradley and Hubbard made the iron castings of the bodies for

Novelty Wall Clocks

Mueller and Son. Other clocks available with moving eyes were a dog, lion, organ grinder, and Santa Claus. Some of these clocks are valued at more than $1,000.

Many of the novelty clocks that use animals in their design, like horses, dogs, birds, squirrels, and cats are pictured in this chapter. The bodies or cases of these clocks are predominately metal, but some wooden examples can also be found.

The Ansonia Clock Company developed many expensive models with a unique twist: a doll swinging on the pendulum. An 1889 catalog shows an Ansonia clock named "Jumper # 3," a thirty-hour, time-only clock with a four-inch dial. It is pictured without a stand and measures fifteen inches high. Caution must be observed when purchasing any of these pendulum swingers because they have been widely reproduced.

In the 1870s, F. Kroeber used this swinging function in two clocks he developed. Both clocks display a child swinging to and fro on the pendulum rod. One of the clocks is bronzed while the other is a combination of pot metal and walnut. During the twentieth century, Mastercrafters produced electric novelty clocks, often depicting children swinging on pendulums.

Seth Thomas, Plymouth Hollow, and G. K. Proctor & Co. teamed up to patent a burglar and fire-detection alarm clock in 1860. A lamp lit up when the alarm sounded. The clock's rosewood case was eleven-and-a-quarter inches high. Seth Thomas also created a thirty-hour ship's bell clock.

Gain's Reminder clock made by Valley Mfg. Co., Muscatine, Iowa, patented March 15, 1921, 4 1/2 x 20" h. $500.

Keebler cuckoo pendulette, molded wood, red & green foliage, 30-hour, time only, spring driven, 5 x 6 1/2" h. $125.

It had a metal case with a bell beneath and struck ship's bells rather than the hours. Waterbury and the Chelsea Clock Company made ship's bell clocks as well. The latter was probably the largest producer of this type of clock, with the widest variety of styles.

Novelty clock manufacturers produced other innovative clocks. For example, the Yale Clock Company produced two rectangular tilted clocks on a shared base to help serious chess players time

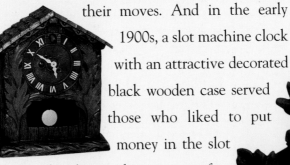

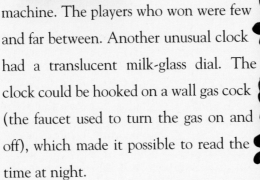

Keebler birdhouse clock w/original box, 30-hour time only, 6 x 7 1/2" h. **$275**.

their moves. And in the early 1900s, a slot machine clock with an attractive decorated black wooden case served those who liked to put money in the slot machine. The players who won were few and far between. Another unusual clock had a translucent milk-glass dial. The clock could be hooked on a wall gas cock (the faucet used to turn the gas on and off), which made it possible to read the time at night.

A novelty Hickory-Dickory-Dock clock shows a white mouse running up the clock. The New Haven Clock Company developed five models of this nursery-rhyme-inspired mouse clock. A Sessions brand clock depicting the same nursery rhyme is illustrated in this chapter.

Two Ferris-wheel clocks that were souvenirs of the Paris 1900 Exposition are pictured in this chapter. As the clock runs, the Ferris wheel turns. The time-only clocks are nearly twelve inches high.

Ansonia's Plato clock is an early version of a

Keebler cuckoo pendulette, molded wood, green colored leaves, 30-hour, time only, spring driven, 3 1/2 x 6" h. **$55**.

digital clock. Eugene L. Fitch, the inventor who patented it in 1902, called it a time indicator. Numbered hour and minute leaves flipped, displaying the correct time. Replicas of this timepiece have been made in Germany.

The Lux Manufacturing Company of Waterbury, Connecticut, began making novelty clocks as a family project prior to World War I. DeLux and Keebler are two names often found on its timepieces. Current events and comic characters often provided the inspiration for their amusing clocks. Lux clocks include the following scenes: a butcher chopping meat while a cat watches; a monkey climbing a fence while an organ grinder turns a crank; and two men drinking over a beer barrel.

Manufacturers kept cost to a minimum by using synthetic materials such as compressed molded wood and a synthetic marble called "Marblesque." Lux's pendulettes have been produced in large numbers and incorporate unusual objects for the pendulums. For example, on the Dixie Boy Pendulette, the boy's necktie forms the pendulum, which swings back and forth as his eyes roll from side to side.

Keebler pendulette, molded wood, spread winged eagle at the top, green leaves, 30-hour, time only, spring driven, 4 x 5" h. **$55**.

Keebler cuckoo pendulette, molded wood, 30-hour, time only, spring driven, 4 x 5" h. **$55**.

Keebler cuckoo pendulette, molded wood, green leaves & red flowers, bluebird feeds its babies, 30-hour, time only, spring driven, 4 x 5" h. **$55**.

Lux Christmas wreath wall clock, 3" d., sold for $2.98 in 1930. **$3,000**.

Lux Shmoo clock in its original box, never used; Li'l Abner & Daisy Mae are pictured on the box, 30-hour, time only, spring driven, 4 x 7" h. **$600**.

Lux cuckoo pendulette, molded wood, bird sitting on top, 30-hour, time only, spring driven, 4 x 6" h. **$55**.

Lux cuckoo pendulette, molded wood, green leaves & bluebird, time only, spring driven, 4 x 5" h. **$55**.

Lux cuckoo pendulette, molded wood, bird sitting at the top, 30-hour, time only, spring driven, 4 1/2 x 7" h. **$55**.

Lux cuckoo pendulette w/original box marked, "Lux Pendulette Clock—a Novelty Clock by Lux," 30-hour, time only, spring driven, 4 x 7" h. **$175**.

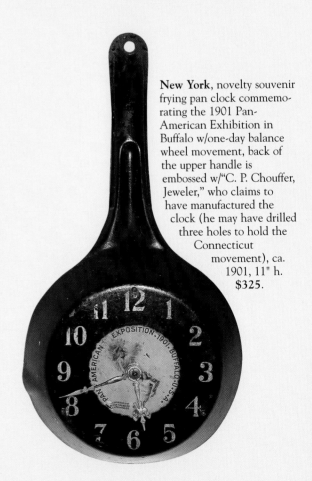

New York, novelty souvenir frying pan clock commemorating the 1901 Pan-American Exhibition in Buffalo w/one-day balance wheel movement, back of the upper handle is embossed w/"C. P. Chouffer, Jeweler," who claims to have manufactured the clock (he may have drilled three holes to hold the Connecticut movement), ca. 1901, 11" h. **$325**.

Sessions wooden Dickory, Dickory Dock clock has a white mouse running up & down the time line, eight-day time only, 35" h. **$1,000**.

Novelty Shelf Clocks

Ansonia metal novelty clocks w/jeweled settings. Left, "Army" w/rifle supports, antique brass, gilt center, porcelain dial, one-day, time only, 2" dial, 12" h. **$900**.
Right, "Navy" w/oar supports, antique brass, gilt center, porcelain dial, one-day, time only, 2" dial, 12" h. **$850**.

Left, **Ansonia** Plato "Design #2" early digital novelty clock, patented 1903, time only, 6 1/2" h. **$650**.
Right, "Design #4" early digital novelty clock, patented 1903, time only, 6 1/2" h. **$650**.

Ansonia "Bee" clock shown w/its original shipping tin, time only, ca. 1890, 2" dial **$175**.

Ansonia "Eva" novelty shelf clock w/brass surround, patented 1892, porcelain dial, beveled mirror, eight-day time only, 8 x 9 1/2" h. **$800.**

Ansonia brass jeweled novelty clocks. Left, "The Harp" 30-hour, time only, 1 1/2" dial, 9" h. **$800.**
Right, "The Token" porcelain dial, gilt center, two cupids within heart design, 30-hour, time only, 1 1/2" dial, 5 1/2" h. **$600.**

Ansonia "Novelty #23 Peacock" w/embossed metal surround & appendages, 30-hour, time only, 2" dial, 7 1/2" h. **$700**.
Right, "Novelty #20 Birds" metal, 30-hour, time only, 2" dial, 4 1/2" h. **$600**.

Ansonia "Jumper #1" 30-hour, time only, 4" dial, 15 1/2" h. **$1,800**.
Right, "Jumper #2" 30-hour, time only, 4" dial, 14 1/2" h. **$1,750**.

Ansonia "Novelty #34" also called "The Advertiser" because there is space for ads above & below the dial, 30-hour, time only, 7" h. **$650**.
Right, Ansonia "Novelty #15" w/owl supporting clock, 30-hour, time only, 2" dial, 6" h. **$650**.

Ansonia metal man beating time, 30-hour, time only, 2" dial, 5" h. **$1,250.**
Right, Ansonia "Novelty #48" of children sledding, 30-hour, time only, 6 x 6 3/4" h. **$1,000.**

Ansonia "The Sonnet" brass framed novelty shelf clock, w/knight's head on velvet background, eight-day time only, tandem spring drive, 20 1/2" h. **$2,000.**

Ansonia metal novelty clocks. Left, "Simmons Liver Regulator" on horseshoe surround, 30-hour, time only, 6" h. **$500.**
Right, "Pearl" 30-hour, time only, 4" d. dial, 6 1/2" h. **$250.**

Ansonia "Square Pirate" clock w/original cardboard box, 4 x 4" h. **$75**.

Ansonia "Train Novelty #44" patented April 23, 1878, 30-hour, time only, 2" dial, 7 3/4" h. **$750**. Right, Ansonia "Cat Novelty #52" 30-hour, time only, 2" dial, 9" h. **$1,100**.

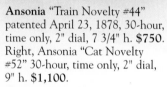

Ansonia brass novelty clocks, Left: "Swing #1" doll, 30-hour, time only, 4" dial, 11 1/2" h. **$2,400**. Right, "Swing #2" doll, 30-hour, time only, 4" dial, 8" h. **$1,500**.

Ansonia "Twins" 30-hour, time only, movement patented
March 27, 1877, 3" dial, 10 1/2" h. **$600**.
Right, Ansonia "The Jug" 30-hour, time only, 3" dial, 10" h.
$225.

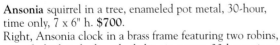

Ansonia squirrel in a tree, enameled pot metal, 30-hour,
time only, 7 x 6" h. **$700**.
Right, Ansonia clock in a brass frame featuring two robins,
one of which is feeding the babies in a nest, 30-hour, time
only, 5 1/2 x 7" h. **$350**.

Ansonia metal bouncing doll, patent date
on dial is Dec. 14, 1886, original German
doll, 15 1/2" h. **$1,750**.

Ansonia brass trotter novelty clock, 30-hour, time only, 10 1/2 x 6 1/2" h. **$750**.

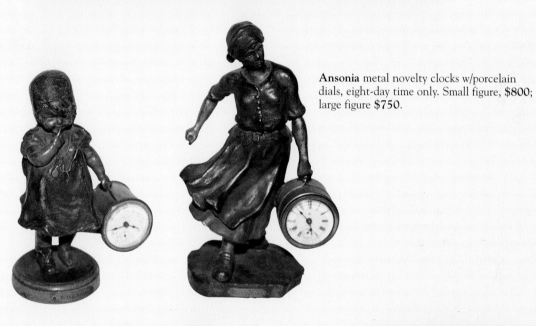

Ansonia metal novelty clocks w/porcelain dials, eight-day time only. Small figure, **$800**; large figure **$750**.

Ansonia brass Cupid riding a snail, 30-hour, time only, 5" h. **$300**.
Right, Ansonia brass baby holding a fan, 30-hour, time only, 5" h. **$475**.

Ansonia cast-iron black enamel novelty mantel clock, w/a ship's brass wheel rotating as the escapement moves, seen in 1894 catalog, 15 x 18 3/4" h. **$2,200**.

Ansonia metal castle novelty clock, time only, 14" h. **$475**.

Ansonia metal ship novelty clocks w/cupid figure on each, 30-hour, time only. The middle ship is 13" h. & other two are 9" h. **$375**.

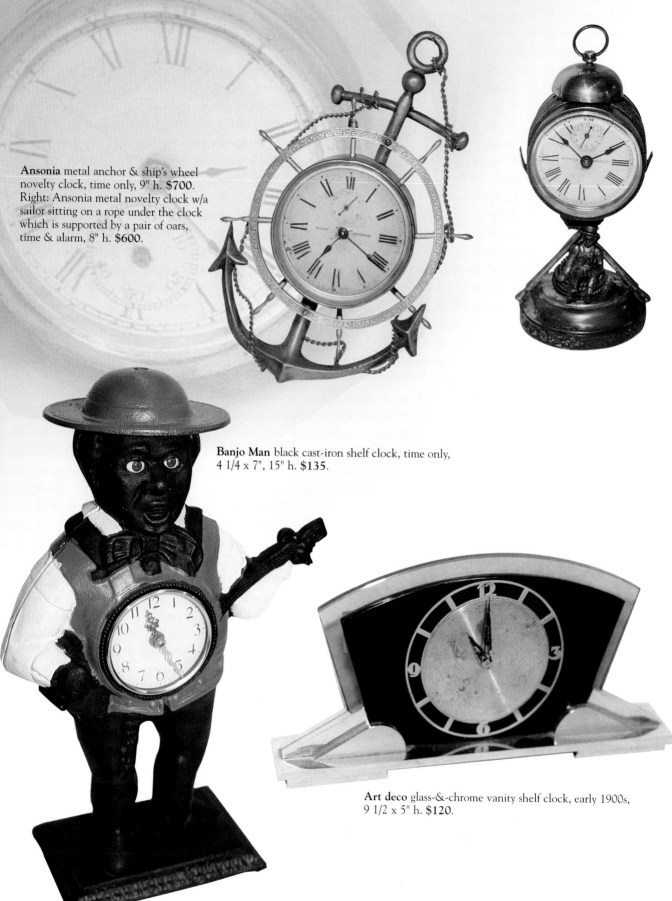

Ansonia metal anchor & ship's wheel
novelty clock, time only, 9" h. **$700**.
Right: Ansonia metal novelty clock w/a
sailor sitting on a rope under the clock
which is supported by a pair of oars,
time & alarm, 8" h. **$600**.

Banjo Man black cast-iron shelf clock, time only,
4 1/4 x 7", 15" h. **$135**.

Art deco glass-&-chrome vanity shelf clock, early 1900s,
9 1/2 x 5" h. **$120**.

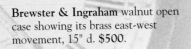

Brewster & Ingraham walnut open case showing its brass east-west movement, 15" d. **$500**.

J. E. Buerk, Boston, made the first time clock, patented 1861, brass w/leather case, 3 1/2" d. **$700**.

Columbia Fine Products, LaSalle, Illinois, Woody's Café animated shelf clock, made by 4" d., 18" h. **$175**.

John Deere pocket watch
w/revolving second indicator,
made in the 1930s, 2" d.
$200.

Forestville wooden vanity shelf clock
w/temperature gauge & brass face,
20th c., 8 1/2 x 5" h. **$40.**

W. L. Gilbert wooden religious mass clock, 5 x 6" h. **$150**.

Kline & Company, New York, "#602" chronometer in a wooden case, fusee operated, ca. 1830, 7 1/4 x 7 1/2" h. **$2,500**.

F. Kroeber pot metal & walnut "Angel Swing" novelty parlor clock, reconditioned case, eight-day time only, ca. 1876, 19 1/2" h. **$2,800**.

F. Kroeber bronzed novelty clock w/Kroeber movement, girl swings to & fro by using Kroeber's double escapement wheel on the pendulum rod, Egyptian lady's head above dial, eight-day time only, 5 x 19" h. **$2,000**.

F. Kroeber "Sheffield" walnut miniature novelty shelf clock, time only, ca. 1890, 20" h. **$175**.

F. Kroeber owl novelty clock, glass eyes, 30-hour, time & alarm, 6 x 10" h. **$475**.

Lux "Happy Days" clock, showing two drinkers standing next to a "3 Point 2" beer barrel, 30-hour, time only, 4 x 4" h. **$250**.

Lux "Show Boat" clock w/paddle wheel that turns, 30-hour, time only, 5 x 4 1/2" h. **$175**.

Lux composition (molded) shelf clock in shape of church,
13 x 14" h. **$75**.

Lux novelty shelf clock, showing fireplace scene w/turning spinning wheel, 30-hour, time & alarm, 4 1/2 x 5" h. $150.

Lux vanity clock, time only, 7 x 4" h. $85.

New Haven fan novelty clock w/brass stand & decorations, porcelain & brass dial, 30-hour, time only, 13 x 8" h. $850.

New Haven ball watch hanging on eagle stand w/onyx base, 30-hour, time only, 9" h. **$1,100.**

New Haven brass dresser clock, porcelain dial, 3" d., time only. **$100.**

Oxford Metal Spinning Co., Inc. porcelain-&-brass electric shelf clock, featuring horse & cart, mid-1900s, 22 x 10 1/2" h. **$297.**

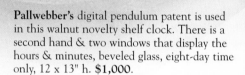

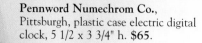

Pennword Numechrom Co., Pittsburgh, plastic case electric digital clock, 5 1/2 x 3 3/4" h. **$65.**

Pallwebber's digital pendulum patent is used in this walnut novelty shelf clock. There is a second hand & two windows that display the hours & minutes, beveled glass, eight-day time only, 12 x 13" h. **$1,000.**

Sentinola kitchen call, like a timer, tells when cooking is done, 7 1/2 x 7" h. **$50.**

Sessions wooden case vanity electric shelf clock, mid-1900s, 9 x 7" h. **$40**.

Sessions wooden-framed shelf clock, 8 x 7" h. **$25**.

Sessions windmill shelf clock, 9 x 11" h. **$70**.

Sundial wall or shelf clock, 5" d., 2 1/2" h. **$35**.

Timby Solar walnut novelty shelf clock w/a world globe that rotates to indicate the hours, base dial rotates to register the minutes, time only, only 600 of these clocks were made, 14 x 27" h. **$5,500**

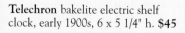

Telechron bakelite electric shelf clock, early 1900s, 6 x 5 1/4" h. **$45**

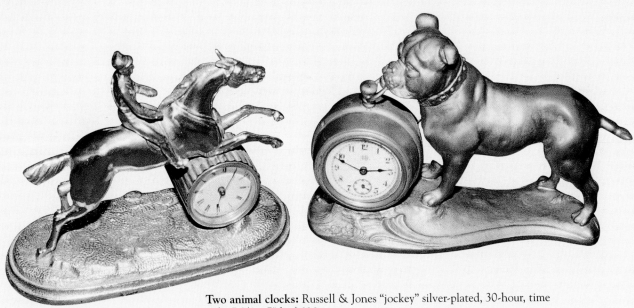

Two animal clocks: Russell & Jones "jockey" silver-plated, 30-hour, time only, 7 3/4 x 7" h. **$600**.
Right, Jennings Brothers Mfg. Co. bulldog, gilt finish, patented Jan. 13, 1891, Bridgeport, Connecticut, 30-hour, time only, 8 x 6" h. **$450**.

Two small automobile clocks installed in homemade walnut frames. Waltham, the taller of the two, 5 x 9" h. **$125**.
Smaller clock made by Phinney Walker Co., Inc., New York, 4 1/2 x 6 3/4" h. **$95**.

United Clock Corp. Brooklyn, N.Y., covered wagon & horses, gilded electric clock, 5 x 19", 10" h., **$225**.

United Electric bronzed table clock featuring pirates, 13 x 13" h. **$75**.

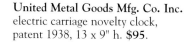

United Metal Goods Mfg. Co. Inc. electric carriage novelty clock, patent 1938, 13 x 9" h. **$95**.

Unknown maker w/Herschede movement American shelf clock, seven jewels, eight-day time only, ca. 1900, 7" d. **$250**.

Unknown maker reproduction of Flying Pendulum novelty clock, original patent date was 1883, 7 x 10" h. **$100**.

Unknown maker metal Ferris wheel novelty clock, souvenir of the Paris 1900 Exposition (printed on tablet), as the clock runs, the Ferris wheel turns, time only, 5 x 11 1/2" h. **$1,200**.

Unknown maker electrically operated plastic
windmill shelf clock w/moving blades, time only,
ca. 1940, 8 1/2" h. **$100**.

Another example of a Ferris wheel clock,
this one w/a plain tablet.
$1,200.

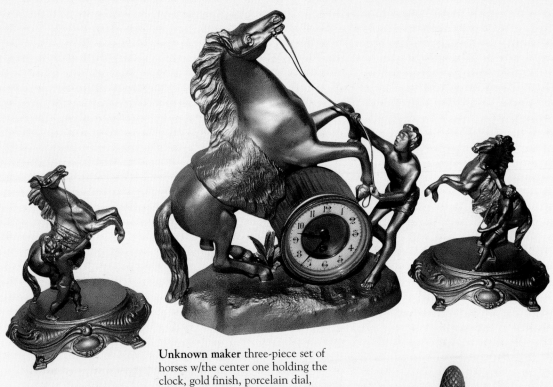

Unknown maker three-piece set of horses w/the center one holding the clock, gold finish, porcelain dial, beveled glass, eight-day time only, ca. 1890 12 x 15 1/2" h. **$650**.

Unknown maker brass Masonic emblem novelty desk clock, time only, ca. 1910, 6 1/2" h. **$225**.

Unknown maker mahogany-finished four-column novelty shelf clock, porcelain dial, time only, 6 1/2" d. dial, 13" h. **$250**.

Waterbury wooden & metal novelty clock showing boy w/saw, patented Jan. 13, 1891, 30-hour, time only, 8 1/2 x 10 1/2" h. **$650**.

Waterbury walnut stained shelf clock w/a hand that goes up & down & rotates at the top & bottom to show time on this elongated dial, eight-day time only, 13 x 15" h. **$550**.

E. N. Welch "Rosebud" clock w/an angel & flowers inscribed on the brass clock surround, 30-hour, time only, 6 x 7" h. **$400**.

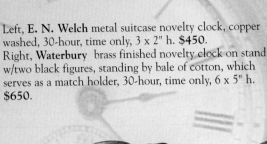

Left, **E. N. Welch** metal suitcase novelty clock, copper washed, 30-hour, time only, 3 x 2" h. **$450**.
Right, **Waterbury** brass finished novelty clock on stand w/two black figures, standing by bale of cotton, which serves as a match holder, 30-hour, time only, 6 x 5" h. **$650**.

E. N. Welch metal suitcase novelty clock, copper finished, 30-hour, time only, 3 x 3" h. **$300**.

E. N. Welch nickel-plated novelty shelf clock, time only, 3 x 2" h. **$250**. Right, novelty clock shaped like a watch, souvenir from 1893 Chicago World's Fair, 30-hour, time only, 3" d. Inscription on back reads: "Landing of Columbus in America October 12th 1492" **$375**.

E. N. Welch jewel novelty clocks. Left: amber, patented 1881, 30-hour, time only, 4 x 4" h. **$275**. Right: crystal, 30-hour, time only, 4 x 4" h. **$225**.

E. N. Welch jeweled shelf clocks w/60-second hands, time only. Center clock, 7" d. **$150**; amber clock, 4 x 4" h. **$200**; clear clock, 4 x 4" h. **$150**.

Year Clock Company, New York, mahogany case novelty clock that runs a year, patented 1903, 4" dial **$650**.

Chapter 9
Foreign Clocks

A number of European countries, including France, Austria, Germany, Great Britain, Italy, Netherlands, Scandinavia, Spain, and Switzerland made important contributions to the clock industry. However, three nations—France, Germany, and Great Britain—were the definite leaders.

In France, for example, the guild system that developed during the sixteenth century set standards for clockmakers. When the clockmakers' guild was incorporated in 1544, it began regulating the conduct of shops and protecting the rights and privileges of its members. For instance, it gave its members the right to work in silver and gold. With the guild's backing, workers produced the elaborate wood and metal cases that became an accepted French style.

Notable French clockmakers included Ferdinand Berthoud, who worked during the eighteenth century and produced the skeleton clock that is now exhibited in the British Museum. Andre Charles Boulle was another prominent clockmaker who specialized in clock designs. His works were of superb quality, and the phrase "Boulle Work" was given to his particular style of marquetry.

Another clockmaker who lived from the early eighteenth century to its end was Abraham-Louis Brequet. Many consider him the most famous French clockmaker of all time. Most of his work was luxurious and, because of its high quality, very costly.

Eighteenth-century French designs included marble clocks, pillar clocks, and statue or figural clocks. The case designs became an integral part of the clocks' character, and at times, it took several workers to complete them. Woodworkers created cases, stoneworkers produced a vast variety of marble designs, and other workers were employed to cast, finish, and gild the metal applications. With all this expertise, it was small wonder the cases attracted so much attention.

The French taste for ornate clocks continued into the twentieth century. At that time, the clockmaker Frederic Japy, who was considered the father of the French horological industry of the ninteenth century, developed factories for the production of his clock works. In the late 1800s, his factories employed about three thousand workers to produce unfinished movements. With this huge labor force, untold numbers of clock movements were produced annually.

No one is quite sure where the mechanical clock was invented, but it seems likely that it was somewhere in the area where Germany, Switzerland, Italy, and France share borders. A painting made about 1565 depicts a clock dial in a tower, and old German drawings and pictures show towers with

British Unified Clock Company walnut parlor clock, eight-day time & strike, early 1900s, 13 3/4 x 17 1/2" h. $500.

English Eureka Clock Co. Ltd., London, wood-case battery-powered shelf clock, patented 1906, time only, 7 x 8", 13 1/4" h. $2,500.

dials. Credit for the design and development of smaller clocks should be attributed to Peter Henlein of Nuremberg, who manufactured small portable clocks. Augsburg clockmakers developed animated clocks in which mechanical humans and animals performed unusual movements. This environment created a market for workers to specialize in creating and decorating automatic clocks.

When Nuremberg and Augsburg began declining as clock centers, clockmaking moved south to the Black Forest area, where workers made clocks with simpler designs. These clocks were in great demand in the early nineteenth century because they were affordable to German citizens with lower incomes. When cheaper imported American clocks began outselling Black Forest models, German clockmakers successfully copied American styles, producing higher profits than ever before.

Germans stopped copying American clocks, however, when they created more of their own original designs. The Vienna regulator, available in both a weight- and spring-driven model, emerged as the dominant style. The bob of the regulator was engraved with the letters R/A, which means retard/advance.

Gustav Becker, who lived from 1819 to 1885, built clock factories, which helped revitalize the German clock industry. Other clockmakers, encouraged by his success as sales soared, followed suit by creating their own businesses. Soon,

English Eureka Clock Co., Ltd., London, mahogany-case thouand-day electric clock w/porcelain face, time only, 4 1/2 x 8", 11" h. **$1,500**.

English fusee shelf clock, often called a striking skeleton, time only, ca. 1820, 6 x 10", 11" h. **$1,000**.

however, all clock factories were combined under the name Gustav Becker. Later in 1926, Becker merged with Junghans. The Junghans firm was significant because it adopted American mass production techniques. Becker's life marked a period when the American and German clock industries were vying for leadership.

The Vienna regulator produced great success for Austrian clockmakers, as they established new sales records around the world in the late 1800s. Other Austrian clocks were popular as well. One example is the Baroque bracket clock (circa 1750), copied from a British example. Another is a metal wall clock with a painted dial, a single hand, and a "cowtail" pendulum. The unusual pendulum, dating to the early eighteenth century, is short and moves in front of the dial. A third example is an elaborate "aged" bronzed elephant holding a gilt bronzed clock. Its movement and case were designed by different clockmakers. The clock is on display in the Victoria and Albert Museum, London, England. Also favored were a mantel clock with several pillars that supported the movement and dials, and a wall clock with exposed weights.

The history of clockmaking in Great Britain is not as clear as it is in other European nations, but turret clocks were built by the late thirteenth century. These huge structures could be seen at Canterbury in 1286; Westminster, London, in 1288; and St. Paul's, London, in 1292. Several

English fusee shelf clock, w/open escapement & brass fittings visible, time only, ca. 1820, 7 x 12", 15" h. **$1,200**.

English fusee w/inlaid mahogany case, eight-day time only, ca. 1820, 4 x 6", 9 1/2" h. **$350**.

hundred years later, public clocks were present in other population centers of Great Britain.

English clockmakers continued to make larger and more sophisticated clocks, such as the turret, long-case, lantern, table, mantel, and bracket models, which were sold to wealthier citizens. However, it was the English horologists' constant effort to perfect the chronometer, a very accurate timekeeper, that kept the English dominant in the clock industry. The strength of the English clockmaking trade is evident from the vast number of horologists—over two thousand—who practiced their craft from the early 1600s to the late 1800s.

Both England and Holland are credited with creating the pendulum in the mid-seventeenth century. British inventor Robert Hook contributed another development—the balance wheel. Also credited to English inventors or horologists are the compensation pendulum, marine and pocket chronometers, and Thomas Mudge's lever escapement. English clockmakers Thomas Tompion, Daniel Quare, Edward East, and the Knibbses created a pure English style in long-case, bracket, and lantern clocks. An example of the latter, a thirty-hour lantern clock with alarm, circa 1640, is on display in the British Museum, London. In addition to this unusual clock, examples of the table clock of 1665 and the turret clock of 1834 are on exhibit there.

The decline of the English clock industry began

English mahogany two-weight, five-tube grandfather clock, 25 x 90" h. **$7,500**.

English Mercer ship's clock in maple case, three-day, 7 1/2 x 7 1/2", 7" h. **$1,200**.

when England started importing large numbers of very inexpensive, but reliable, clocks from Connecticut, and relatively inexpensive clocks from Germany and Austria. Ironically, the English, once world's leader in clockmaking, have no prominent names, as the French do with the name Japy, the Germans with Becker, or the Americans with Gilbert. The English clockmakers' emphasis on quality, rather than quantity caused their decline, yet it also permanently secured an excellent reputation for those that survived.

English regulator walnut wall clock w/porcelain & brass dial, eight-day time & strike, 13 x 39" h. **$2,500.**

English walnut wall clock, eight-day time & strike, 15 x 36" h. **$1,800.**

French 15-day clock w/four pillars &
gild & color decorations on clock
frame, time & strike, 5 1/2 x 9 1/2",
19" h. **$695**

French B. Apres – L – Angelus brass wall
clock, eight-day time only, 6 x 14" h.
$250.

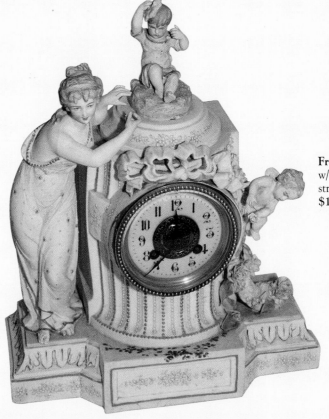

French bisque shelf clock
w/carved figures, eight-day time &
strike, ca. early 1900s, 12 x 14" h.
$1,500.

French brass-case alarm clock, eight-day, 4" d. **$400**.

French castle alarm, three-day time only, 9 x 10" h. **$300**.

French (probably) bronze statue clock, , eight-day time & strike, 20 x 27" h. **$3,495**.

French Endura brass-case vanity shelf clock, early 1900s, 3 1/2 x 5" h. **$25**.

French iron statue clock featuring a woman & child, eight-day time & strike, 6 x 15", 24" h. **$2,095**.

French gilded iron-statue clock, eight-day time & strike, late 1800s, 10 1/2 x 16" h. **$725**.

French Japy silk-string mantel clock w/Napoleon featured on the top, eight-day time & strike, ca. 1800, 4 x 11", 17 1/2" h. **$1,800**.

French Japy gilt-coated silk-string mantel clock displayed at the Paris Exposition Grande in 1855, eight-day time & strike, 13 x 16" h. **$400**.

French Japy ornate oak shelf clock w/brass decorations, eight-day time & strike, 8 x 9", 13" h. **$700**.

French Limoges porcelain shelf clock, 30-hour, ca. 1880, 8 1/2 x 10 1/2" h. **$300**.

French mahogany wall clock, eight-day time & strike w/Westminster chimes, 16 1/2 x 22 1/2" h. **$795.**

French mantel clock marked A. Chaple, Paris, w/brass & marble appointments, eight-day time & strike, ca. 1890s, 12 x 22" h. **$900.**

French Marti black mantel clock w/marble inlay, porcelain face & open escapement, eight-day time & strike, 5 x 9 1/2", 17" h. **$400.**

French marble mantel statue clock w/removable female statue, fancy brass & porcelain dial, eight-day time & strike, ca. 1890, **$795.**

French Marti mahogany-case balloon clock, eight-day time & strike, 5 x 7", 13" h. **$350.**

French Marti cast-iron statue clock w/spring-wind mechanism, eight-day time & strike, 15 x 14" h. **$450.**

French Marti cast-iron statue clock w/silk-thread suspension, eight-day time & strike, 17 x 17" h. **$750.**

French novelty clock w/copper finish & porcelain face, decorated w/reproduction Roman coins around its 8" d. **$250**.

French porcelain base lighthouse clock w/barometer, eight-day time only, ca. 1787, 7" d., 18" h. **$1,800**.

French porcelain shelf clock under glass dome w/unusual silk string movement, 8 x 16" h. **$6,500**.

French shelf alarm clock from the Paris Exposition, 1889, time only, 5" d. **$350**.

French S. Lovens metal statue clock w/bronze finish, 13 x 29" h. **$3,000**.

French shelf clock w/alabaster sides, marbleized pillars & brass decorations, eight-day time & strike, ca. 1820, 5 x 9 1/2", 16" h. **$400**.

French three piece clock set w/two flanking side pieces 19" h., eight-day time & strike, 21 x 29" h., 5" d. face. **$5,400**.

French statue clock, 16 x 25" h. **$2,495**.

French three piece clock set w/cast-iron mantel clock on its marble base, 15 x 24" h. & matching pair of urns 5" d., 6 1/2 x 23" h. & 5" porcelain dial. Gilded figures of child & lady support the clock, eight-day time & strike, 15" x 24" h. **$2,895**.

German alarm clock that swivels on base, 3 1/2" d., 4" h. **$45**.

French walnut wall clock w/barometer & thermometer, w/Roman numerals on porcelain, 14 x 35" h. **$750**.

German anniversary clocks. Left, clock marked Schatz on face, 7 1/2" d. at base, 12" h. **$285**; Right, clock made in West Germany & marked Knundo on face, 8" d., 12" h. **$185**.

German Gustav Becker walnut wall clock w/two weights & porcelain dial, eight-day time & strike, ca. 1890, 14 1/2 x 48" h. **$900.**

German Gustav Becker mahogany two-weight wall clock w/a porcelain face & small second hand, eight-day time & strike, late 1800s, 16 1/2 x 52" h. **$3,000.**

German Black Forest composition & wood-finish hanging cuckoo clock, 30-hour, 10 x 12" h. ca. 1975, **$125.**

German Black Forest walnut shelf clock w/flower carvings & eagle holding a snake in its bill, 18 x 23" h. **$3,800**.

German clock depicting chalk figure at well & inscription that reads, "Return from Work," 30-hour time only, ca. 1920, 10 x 23 1/2" h. **$140**.

German Black Forest oak wall clock w/deer carving at the top, eight-day time & strike, 11" d. face, hands missing. **$4,800**.

German enamelware nursery rhyme clock, eight-day, 9 1/2 x 9" h. **$500**.

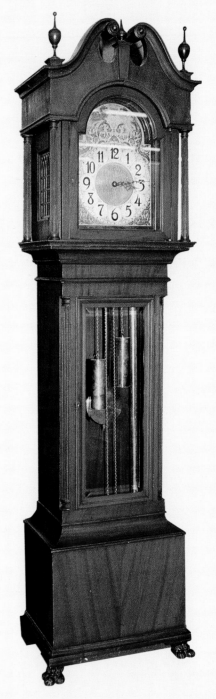

German grandfather floor clock, 19th c., 22 x 92" h. **$3,900**.

German Fredrich Kilmer shelf clock w/oak base, brass dial, & gilded-iron surround, 4 x 8", 12" h. **$300**.

German Junghans bronze carriage clock, eight-day time & strike, 4 3/4 x 5 1/2", 6" h. **$105**.

German Junghans metal carriage clock, winds & plays music & has an alarm & small second hand, ca. 1870, 5 1/2 x 7" h. **$70**.

German Junghans swinging arm statue clock, time only, 5" d. base, 13 1/2" h. **$400**.

German Junghans oak carriage clock w/porcelain face, eight-day, 2 x 4", 6" h. **$80**.

German Junghans oak case shelf clock w/brass legs, eight-day time only, ca. 1820, 4 x 6", 10 1/2" h. **$250**.

Junghans

German music box alarm,
3 1/4 x 4 1/2" h. **$55**.

German porcelain mantel clock featuring
young girl, turn of century, 30-hour time only,
6 x 7" h. **$160**.

German Royal Beyreuth
Bavarian rose tapestry shelf
clock, face & works made in the
U. S. A., patented Oct. 8, 1907,
30-hour, 4 1/4 x 4 1/2" h.
$1,500.

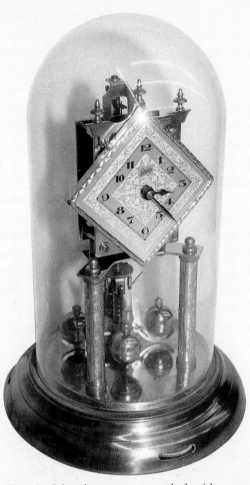

German Schmid Sheukler Jr. metal flowerpot clock w/jeweled movement, 3" d., 7 3/4" h. **$400**.

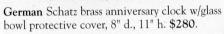

German Schatz brass anniversary clock w/glass bowl protective cover, 8" d., 11" h. **$280**.

German Schmid green & red plastic case, four-jewel shelf clocks, eight-day, ca. 1950, 4 x 8 1/2" h. **$100 each**.

German Schmid red plastic case, four-jewel shelf clock, eight-day, ca. 1950, 4 x 8 1/2" h. $100.

German Schmid plastic case wall clock, time only, ca. 1950, 14 1/2" h. $100.

German Schmid brass-case shelf clock w/porcelain face & pendulum visible through base opening, eight-day, 4 x 7" h. $100.

German Vienna medium-size regulator, eight-day time & strike, 10 x 39" h. **$400**.

German Vienna regulator w/three weights & two-piece porcelain dial, 16 x 50" h. **$1,500**.

German Schmid eight-day shelf clock, 10" h. **$125**.

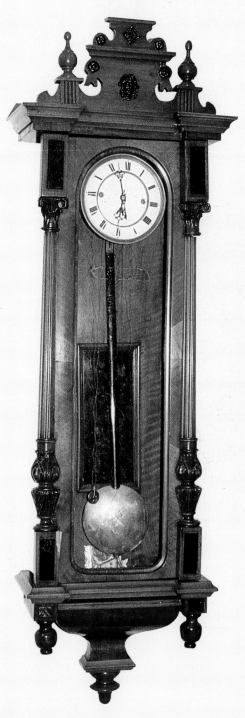

German Vienna regulator, walnut case, w/two weights, 15 x 47" h. **$2,395**.

German Vienna walnut regulator w/three weights, late 1800s, 16 x 56" h. **$3,200**.

Chapter 10
Useful Clock Information

CLOCK CARE

Insuring

Always maintain adequate insurance on your clock. Photograph your clock and write a detailed description of it. Keep a copy of the photo, description, purchase records, and any other pertinent information in a safe place in case of fire, flood, burglary, etc. This will make it much easier to file an insurance claim.

Cleaning

Clean your clock every three to five years. For best results, have it cleaned professionally, but if you do it yourself, first remove the hands, dial, and works. Immerse the works in naptha or kerosene for about thirty minutes, then wipe with a soft cloth and dry with a hair dryer. Clean unpainted glass with glass cleaner to remove all streaks and fingerprints, and dust the case with a soft cloth. Oil the pivots with clock oil, which can be purchased at hobby shops. Apply small drops of oil using the tip of a long needle, then reassemble the clock.

Moving

Before moving a weight-driven or pendulum clock, remove the weight or pendulum to prevent damage.

Move a large clock carefully. Carry it by supporting its weight from underneath. Do not lift it by the top or by other fragile parts. Also, keep the clock as vertical as possible, as strain, twisting, or uneven weight distribution may cause cracking or other damage.

Displaying

Carefully select your clock's location. Keep it away from drafts, basements, outside walls, and heating and ventilating ducts because humidity and temperature extremes can warp wood and affect a clock's accuracy. Also avoid placing a clock in direct sunlight, which may cause the finish to fade or crack.

Be sure your clock is firmly anchored. If placed on a wall, ensure that the support is heavy enough and is attached to a wall stud or a wall anchor.

To keep the clock as accurate as possible, be sure the clock is level front to back and side to side.

Maintaining

Leave all major clock repairs to a professional, but if you choose to work on your clock's movement, first remove weights or pendulum, and disengage springs.

Running

Dedicated clock collectors usually keep their clocks running, if possible. The springs and other moving parts will not wear out. If fact, keeping the moving parts running helps preserve them and maintains the clock's accuracy.

Winding

Because of a series of protective devices called Geneva Stops, you can't overwind your clock.

Establish a regular shedule to wind your clock. Use your normal routine as a reminder. For example, you might want to wind your clock at the beginning of a weekly TV show.

Adjusting

If your clock runs too fast or slow, you can adjust its timing up to five minutes a week by raising or lowering the pendulum bob or adjusting its weights. Weight-driven clocks are generally more accurate than spring-driven models, so they may not require as much adjustment.

The phrase "Lower, slower, higher, sprier" provides a good way to remember how to adjust a pendulum clock. Raising the bob on the pendulum rod shortens the swing so the clock goes faster. Lowering the bob makes the arc longer, which slows the clock.

Learning

Beginning clock collectors can join the National Association of Watch and Clock Collectors (NAWCC) at 514 Poplar Street, Columbia, PA 17512. Fellow members and club activities can be of great help.

Selling

Well-made and maintained antique clocks are valuable and in constant demand. If you prepare your clock for sale properly and ask a fair price, you should have little difficulty selling it. To receive the highest price within your clock's market value, follow the guidelines below:

Make sure your clock looks its best by having it cleaned (see instructions in the Clock Care section above).

Preserve any labels found on a clock case, as they may give horological and historical information that will increase the clock's value.

Have your clock appraised by several reputable dealers and average their values to arrive at a price.

Clocks can be sold through antique shows, antique shops, traditional and online auctions, clock conventions, collector periodicals, and newspaper advertisements.

If you aren't selling in person, be sure to provide color photos that include multiple angles and close-ups of unique features. Also provide a detailed written description of the clock's features and flaws. Be sure to mention what you would consider minor or insignificant flaws. Potential buyers have a right to full disclosure.

As a courtesy (and an extra selling point), include repair history, if known, as well as instructions for operating and cleaning your clock.

HOW CLOCK FEATURES AND CONDITION AFFECT VALUE

If you are considering buying or selling a clock, you should be aware of factors that will likely increase or reduce a clock's value. The amount of increase or decrease of value depends on the individual clock. Consult a professional for an appraisal.

Features that increase value:

1. Unique motion (for example, a girl swinging on a pendulum)
2. Unusual shape (such as an acorn, banjo, or figure-eight clock)
3. Uncommon case material (like marble, onyx, exotic wood veneer, marquetry, or intricately shaped metal)
4. Distinctive strike (quarter hour, half hour, chime, music, and cuckoo)
5. Visible pendulum, escapement, or balance wheel
6. Carved wooden or metal applications on cases
7. Moderate to deeply pressed designs on wooden cases

Conditions that lower value:

1. Worn, replaced, or repainted dials
2. Replaced hands, pendulums, and weights
3. Repaired or replaced movements
4. Damaged, repainted, or replaced glass tablets (panels)
5. Completely refinished cases
6. Faded, stained, or torn labels
7. Repairs to cases, such as replaced veneers and filled holes
8. Repairs made to porcelain and marble clocks

PATENT SERIAL NUMBERS GROUPED IN TEN-YEAR PERIODS

A patent date can help detemine the approximate age of a clock.

Patent Numbers	Years Included
1-1,464	1836-1839
1,465-6,980	1840-1849
6,981-26,641	1850-1859
26,642-98,459	1860-1869
98,460-223,210	1870-1879
223,211-418,664	1880-1889
418,665-640,166	1890-1899
640,167-945,009	1900-1909
945,010-1,326,898	1910-1919
1,326,899-1,742,180	1920-1929
1,742,181-2,185,169	1930-1939
2,185,170-2,492,943	1940-1949
2,492,944-2,919,442	1950-1959

CLOCK ASSOCIATION

The National Association of Watch and Clock Collectors, Inc., or NAWCC, is a national organization for clock and watch collectors that sponsors educational meetings, shows, and seminars for it members.

NAWCC
514 Poplar Street
Columbia, PA 17512

CLOCK MUSEUMS

American Clock & Watch Museum
100 Maple Street

Bristol, Connecticut

Henry Ford Museum
Greenfield Village

Dearborn, Michigan

Greensboro Clock Museum
300 Bellemeade St.

Greensboro, North Carolina

Museum of Clocks and Watches
New York University

Albany, New York

The National Clock and Watch Museum
514 Poplar Street

Box 33

Columbia, Pennsylvania

Old Clock Museum
929 E. Preston

Pharr, Texas

J. Cheney Wells Clock Gallery
Old Sturbridge Village

Sturbridge, Massachusetts

Henry Francis DuPont Winterthur Museum
Winterthur, Delaware

CLOCKS ON EXHIBIT AT THE AMERICAN CLOCK AND WATCH MUSEUM

The following clocks can be found at the American Clock and Watch Museum, Bristol, Connecticut. The clocks are listed in chronological order.

1710	English lantern clock made by Henry Webster, London, England.
1711	English clock with inlaid marquetry case by William Troutbeck, Leeds, England.
1750	Cheney-style wooden tall clock with movement and dial made in eastern Connecticut.
1780	One-day wooden-movement tall clock in pine case made by Alexander T. Willard, at Ashby, Massachusetts.
1790	Connecticut tall clock in cherry case by Thomas Harland, Norwich, Connecticut.
1790	Benjamin Willard tall clock.
1795	Kidney-dial shelf clock in mahogany case by Aaron Willard, Boston, Massachusetts.
1802	Pine-cased clock with one-day wooden movement by Eli Terry, Plymouth, Connecticut.
1810	Eight-day lyre-style wall clock made by Samuel Abbott, Montpelier, Vermont.
1812	One-day wooden tall clock, with painted case grained to simulate expensive wood, made by Thomas & Hoadley, Plymouth, Connecticut.
1814	Tall clock with painted pine case and eight-day wooden movement by Joseph Ives, Bristol, Connecticut.

1815   Eli Terry's earliest shelf clock design in a simple box case.

1816   Gilt French figurine clock with likeness of George Washington, made for American markets by Jean Baptiste Blanc of Paris.

1819   Eli Terry pillar-and-scroll clock.

1820   Pillar-and-scroll clock made by Seth Thomas, Plymouth, Connecticut.

1820   Joseph Ives mirror clock in gilt gesso made in Bristol, Connecticut.

1825   Unsigned gilt presentation-style banjo clock made in Boston, Massachusetts, area.

1826   Joseph Ives Empire-style shelf clock.

1830   Silas Hoadley pillar-and-scroll shelf clock.

1830   One-day wooden-movement clock by E. Terry & Son, Plymouth, Connecticut.

1835   One-day wooden-movement clock by Luman Watson, Cincinnati, Ohio.

1838   Mahogany-veneered shelf clock by the Forestville Manufacturing Company, Bristol, Connecticut.

1839   One-day hour-glass-style clock with wagon spring by Joseph Ives, Plainville, Connecticut.

1845   Fusee spring-driven steeple clock with balance wheel escapement attributed to Silas B. Terry.

1845   Forty-two-inch-tall Empire clock with etched-glass tablets by Forestville Manufacturing Company, Bristol, Connecticut.

1845   One-day, weight-driven, brass-movement clock by Chauncey Jerome, Bristol, Connecticut.

1847   One-day steeple clock with brass springs by Brewster and Ingrahams, Bristol, Connecticut.

1850   Forty-and-a-half-inch-tall Empire-case clock with whistle pipe organ made by Kirk & Todd, Wolcott, Connecticut.

1851   Papier mâché shelf clock with mother-of-pearl inlay and painted decoration. Movement by Chauncey Jerome and case by the Litchfield Manufacturing Company.

1852   Eight-day shelf clock by Brewster & Ingrahams, Bristol, Connecticut.

1853   Thirty-day wagon-spring-powered clock by Atkins, Whiting & Co., Bristol, Connecticut.

1854   Domed candle-stand clock with balance-wheel escapement by Terryville Manufacturing Company, Terryville, Connecticut.

1855   Howard & Davis astronomical regulator with mercury pendulum.

1860   Two-dial calendar clock made by Burwall & Carter, Bristol, Connecticut.

1860   Venetian-style clock with Joseph Ives tin-plate; tin-wheel clock movement by N. L. Brewster, Bristol, Connecticut.

1865   A blinking-eye clock, with Bradley & Hubbard case.

1865   An American Clock Company iron-front clock.

1865   Theodore R. Timby's patent globe clock manufactured by Lewis E. Whiting, Saratoga Springs, New York.

1865   An American Clock Company painted and gilded iron-front clock.

1865   Gilt-column shelf clock with Ives rolling-pinion strap-plated movement made by S. C. Spring & Company, Bristol, Connecticut.

1866   Small OG-case clock with spring-driven movement and label of Chauncey Jerome, Austin, Illinois.

1872   Wall hanging American regulator by E. Howard Watch & Clock Company.

1873   Watchman's regulator made by E. Howard Watch & Clock Company, Boston, Massachusetts.

1875   Ithaca Calendar Clock Company eight-day calendar clock.

1880   William L. Gilbert Clock Company walnut shelf clock.

1880   Ionic-style gilt wall timepiece with alarm made by E. Ingraham Company.

1880   Twenty-four-inch dial "corrugated gilt gallery clock" by E. Ingraham Company, Bristol, Connecticut.

1885   Philosopher shelf clock by Ansonia Clock Company, Brooklyn, New York. Produced until after 1915.

1885   Regulator No. 4 made by William L. Gilbert Clock Company, Winsted, Connecticut.

1890   French-style mantel clock with a bronze figure of St. George and the Dragon.

1890   Waterbury Clock Company mantel clock in black marble case.

1890   "Bee" alarm clock with box by Ansonia Clock Company, Brooklyn, New York.

1901   "Defender" model oak wall clock by Waterbury Clock Company, Waterbury, Connecticut.

1901   "Monarch" model black-enameled-case mantel clock with painted marbleized wood columns by E. Ingraham Company, Bristol, Connecticut.

1905   "Dewey" model oak kitchen clock made by E. Ingraham Company, Bristol, Connecticut.

1910   "Gloria" model swinging-ball clock by Ansonia Clock Company, Brooklyn, New York. Clock and pendulum both swing, pivoting on figurine's hand.

INVENTORS OF CALENDAR CLOCKS

Patent Date	Inventor	Residence
May 17, 1853	John H. Hawes	Ithaca, N.Y.
Sept. 19, 1854	William H. Atkins and Joseph C. Burritt	Ithaca, N.Y.
Nov. 17, 1857	William H. Atkins and Joseph C. Burritt	Ithaca, N.Y.
Jan. 31, 1860	James E. and Eugene M. Mix	Bristol, Conn.
Mar. 5, 1861	Galusha Maranville	Winston, Conn.
Feb. 4, 1862	Benjamin B. Lewis	Bristol, Conn.
Apr. 4, 1862	James E. and Eugene M. Mix	Bristol, Conn.
Jan. 5, 1864	Don J. Mozart, Levi Beach, and Laporte Hubbell	New York, N.Y.
June 21, 1864	Benjamin B. Lewis	Bristol, Conn.
Apr. 18, 1865	Henry B. Horton	Ithaca, N.Y.
Apr. 24, 1866	George B. Owen	New York, N.Y.
Aug. 28, 1866	Henry B. Horton	Ithaca, N.Y.
June 25, 1867	Charles M. Clinton and Lynfred Mood	Ithaca, N.Y.
July 2, 1867	Alfonzo Boardman	Forestville, Conn.
Nov. 11, 1867	Charles M. Clinton and Lynfred Mood	Ithaca, N.Y.
Jan. 7, 1868	Josiah K. Seem	Canton, Pa.
June 16, 1868	William A. Terry	Bristol, Conn.
Dec. 29, 1868	Benjamin B. Lewis	Bristol, Conn.
Jan. 25, 1870	William A. Terry	Bristol, Conn.
Dec. 24, 1872	Josiah K. Seem	Macomb, Ill.
July 13, 1875	Alfred A. Cowles	New York, N.Y.
July 13, 1875	William A. Terry	Bristol, Conn.
Feb. 15, 1876	Randal T. Andrews	Thomaston, Conn.
Dec. 5, 1876	Albert Phelps	Ansonia, Conn.
June 19, 1877	Daniel J. Gale	Sheboygan, Wis.
July 31, 1877	Florence Kroeber	Hoboken, N.J.
Nov. 15, 1881	Benjamin B. Lewis	Bristol, Conn.
Dec. 13, 1881	Josiah K. Seem	Macomb, Ill.
June 12, 1883	Benjamin Franklin	Chicago, Ill.
June 19, 1883	James E. Young	Genoa, N.Y.
Apr. 21, 1885	Daniel J. Gale	Sheboygan, Wis.
July 30, 1889	A. F. Wells	Friendship, N.Y.
Apr. 14, 1891	Henry S. Prentiss	New York, N.Y.
Oct. 9, 1894	Charles W. Feishtinger	Fritztown, Pa.
Nov. 10, 1896	T. W. R. McCabe	Winston, Conn.
July 15, 1902	John I. Peatfield	Arlington, Mass.

CLOCK DESCRIPTIONS AND PRICES
FROM THE 1897 AND 1927 SEARS, ROEBUCK CATALOGS

Alarm Clock

Beacon Luminous. Nickel Alarm Clock, with luminous dial; height, 6 1/2 inches; width, 4 1/4 inches; 4-inch dial, and is manufactured by the New Haven Clock Company of New Haven, Conn.; best grade lever movement. Price, 97c. Note: The dial on the clock is luminous, and will show distinctly the time in the dark. The darker it is the brighter it glows. Price Range: 78c to $2.62

Porcelain Shelf Clock

Boudoir No. 10. Genuine Porcelain Case, ornamented with gilt and colored, hand painted decorations; height, 7 1/8 inches; length 5 3/8 inches; beveled glass, 2-inch silver dial; has fine lever movement made by the Waterbury Clock Company. Price, $2.50. Price Range: $2.15 to $8.25.

Iron Case Shelf Clock

Leona. Very fancy enameled Iron Case, showing variegated blue finish, in imitation of marble, with fancy colored and gilt ornamentations; height, 12 inches; width, 9 1/4 inches; 6-inch white or gilt dial; fine eight-day movement made by the New Haven Clock Company; strikes hours and half hours on cathedral gong bell. Price: $5.95. Price Range: $5.90 to $7.90.

Mantel Clock

Fresno. Very fine polished wood case, in imitation of black onyx, fancy gilt engraving, marbleized columns, with gilt bronze bases and caps, fancy sash; height, 10 3/8 inches; length, 16 inches; dial, 5 1/2 inches; fine eight-day movement; made by the Waterbury Clock Company, strikes hours and halves on cathedral gong bell. American white dial, Roman figures, or American gilt dial with Arabic figures. Price: $5.40. Price Range: $4.40 to $6.30.

Statue Clock

Knight. Elaborate gilt bronze case, with very fancy engravings and scroll decorations, ornamented with a fine statue of a bugler; very fancy sash, with fine visible escapement; height, 15 inches; width, 15 inches; has fine eight-day movement; made by the Ansonia Clock Company; strikes hours and halves on beautiful cathedral gong bell. Price: $14.85.

Oak Kitchen Clock

Clarence. Fancy Cabinet Clock, 22 1/2 inches high; dial, 6 inches; made in oak only; beautifully carved and ornamented; fine eight-day movement; made by the Ansonia Clock Company; strikes hours and halves on wire bell. Price: $2.75. Price Range: $2.00 to $3.90.

Walnut Parlor Clock

Buffalo. Fancy Cabinet Clock in solid black walnut only; very fancy ornamented and carved case; height, 26 7/8 inches; dial, 8 inches; fitted with fine eight-day movement; made by the Waterbury Clock Company; strikes hours and halves on wire bell with calendar. Price: $3.70. Price Range: $2.00 to $6.15.

Perpetual Calendar Shelf Clock

Fine solid walnut or oak case, elegantly carved, height, 24 inches, dial, 6 inches. This clock is made by the Waterbury Clock Company; has fine eight-day, hour and half-hour strike movements, with cathedral gong bell and calendar. The calendar is perpetual with a 6-inch dial, showing the day of the week, the month, and day of the month; is guaranteed to be thoroughly reliable and accurate. Price: $5.25.

Weight Clock

This is the genuine old reliable Seth Thomas weight clock, made by the Seth Thomas Clock Company of Thomaston, Conn. The case has rosewood or walnut finish, with one-day weight strike movement; height 25 1/2 inches. Price $5.20.

Octagon Lever Wall Clock

Has oak, walnut, or cherry veneered octagon case or round nickel case; movement is patent lever, is made by the Waterbury Clock Company, and is a good reliable timepiece. This clock is especially desirable for offices, schools, churches, etc.; one day, with 4-inch dial, time only. Price: $1.45. Price Range: $1.45 to $4.90.

Ionic or Figure Eight Wall Clock

Saxon. Rosewood veneered case, well finished; height, 22 inches; dial, 10 inches; is made by the New Haven Clock Company, and is especially designed for offices, schools, churches, etc.; eight day; time only. Price: $3.40.

Short Drop Octagon Wall Clock

Has solid oak or fine veneered case; movement is made by the Waterbury Clock Company and is thoroughly reliable. Is designed for offices, schools, or churches. Eight day, 10-inch dial; time only. Price: $3.45. Price Range $3.45 to $4.40.

Long Drop Octagon Wall Clock

Regulator. Has solid oak or handsome veneered and very fine finished case. Height, 32 inches, with 12-inch dial; has very fine eight-day movement, with calendar; made by the Waterbury Clock Company; has wood pendulum rod, which is not affected by changes in temperature, and is a very fine timepiece; makes a very fine office clock or regulator. Price: $5.85.

Wall Clock

Bruce. Oak, walnut, or cherry case, beautifully carved and turned ornaments. Height, 38 1/4 inches; width, 14 3/4 inches; dial, 8 inches; has fine eight-day movement with wood pendulum rod, which is not affected by changes in temperature; made by the Waterbury Clock Company, and is a very fine timepiece. Price: $6.70.

Cuckoo Wall Clock

These clocks are largely in use in Europe and have of late years become very popular in the United States. The clock is quite a novelty, but is thoroughly practical and is certainly a very interesting and pretty ornament in any home. The clock is fitted with a solid brass movement, cut steel pinions, and has two copper finished fancy iron weights. The height of the case is 19 inches, width 13 inches, made of fancy carved German walnut, ebonized ornaments, has white bone hands and figures. Price: $5.50.

(The little door above the dial opens every half hour; a bird appears, flaps its wings, and calls cuckoo, once for half hours and as many times as it is necessary to denote the time on the hours. Before the cuckoo has called the hours, the clock strikes the hours in the regular way.)

Celluloid Shelf Clock

Boudoir Clock. Amber color celluloid, with green color front. Dial, 3 1/4 x 1 7/8 inches, length, 7 7/8 inches, height, 4 3/4 inches. Thirty-hour movement. Not an alarm clock. Price: $3.75. Price Range: $2.35 to $3.75.

Compressed Wood Shelf Clock

Here's the newest clock on the market. The case represents a beautiful bungalow in natural colors; even the foliage is colored to represent nature. It is practically indestructible; made of highly compressed wood pulp compound; carefully enameled in natural colors. The clock runs thirty hours with one winding. Does not alarm. Length, 9 3/4 inches; 5 1/2 inches high. Price: $2.95. Price Range: $2.95 to $3.45.

Tambour Shelf Clock

The Chevalier. Finished in rich mahogany, two-tone inlaid effect. 21 1/2 inches long and 9 5/8 inches high. Silvered dial is 6 inches in diameter with raised bronzed finish numerals. Louis XIV style hands. Price: $6.68. Price Range: $6.68 to $27.75.

Banjo or Willard Clock

This popular clock is as accurate as it is beautiful. Hand rubbed mahogany finish. 35 1/2 inches high and 10 1/8 inches wide at the widest part. Glass is decorated with decalcomania ornamentations. An attractive 6-inch silvered dial. Louis XIV style hands. An excellent eight-day pendulum movement ensures accuracy. Strikes hours and half hours in sweet tone cathedral gong. Price: $13.90.

Glossary

Acorn Clock: A clock whose shape resembles that of an acorn.

Adamantine: A patented colored celluloid applied as veneer.

Advertising Clock: A clock used for promotional purposes on which the advertising may be found on the case, dial, or tablet.

Alarm: An attachment that rings or gongs at a selected time.

Animated Clock: A clock that incorporates a lifelike movement typical of an animal or person.

Anniversary Clock: A clock that runs for a full year on a single wind. It is sometimes called a four-hundred-day clock.

Apron: A decorative piece sometimes used to hide construction details. It may be on the bottom of a case or between the legs of a floor or shelf clock.

Arabic Numerals: Figures on a dial written as 1, 2, 3, etc.

Arbor: The axle on which gears and pinions are mounted.

Arc: The path in which a pendulum swings.

Backboard: The inside back of a clock case, where a label frequently was applied.

Balance: The oscillating wheel that, along with the hairspring, regulates the speed of a clock.

Balloon Clock: A bracket clock that is shaped like a hot-air balloon.

Banding: A strip of veneer used for decorating a clock case.

Banjo Clock: The name given to Simon Willard's wall clock, the "Improved Timepiece," because of its shape.

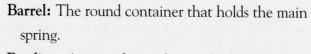

Barrel: The round container that holds the main spring.

Beading: A type of carved or applied molding.

Beat: The ticking sound of a clock. When the ticking is consistently steady, it is "in beat." If it is irregular, it is "out of beat."

Beehive Clock: A clock with a rounded case that bears some resemblance to a beehive; also known as a Gothic clock because its shape is similar to a Gothic arch.

Bevel: A chamfer such as the angled edge on plate glass.

Bezel: A ring of wood or metal that surrounds and holds the glass over the clock dial.

Black Clocks (or Blacks): Clocks made of marble, black iron, or black-enameled wood, popular from about 1880 to 1920.

Black Forest Clock: A clock made in Germany's Black Forest area.

Black Walnut: A common wood used for clock cases.

Blinking Eye Clock: An iron statue clock with moving eyes; also called a winker.

Bob: The weight at the bottom end of a pendulum rod.

Bracket: The part under the box on a Willard banjo clock.

Bracket Clock: The British name for a shelf clock.

Brass Works: A clock mechanism made of brass.

Bushing: The place where the arbor goes through the clock plate for its bearing.

Calendar Clock: A clock that can indicate the day, month, and date, or combinations thereof, as well as the time. A perpetual calendar makes provisions for the various lengths of months and adjusts accordingly; a simple calendar must be

changed manually to accommodate a change from a thirty-day to a thirty-one-day month as well as leap year changes.

Case: The housing for the works of a clock.

Celluloid: A trade name for the first artificial plastic, invented in 1869, that received wide commercial use. Some clock cases in the early 1900s were made of this highly flammable material.

Center Seconds Hand: The hand that is mounted on the center of the dial; also called "sweep second hand."

Chamfer: A sloping or angled edge on wood or plate glass; a bevel.

Chime: The simple melody on the bells or gongs that sounds on the hour, or at the quarter and half hours.

China or Porcelain Clock: A clock with a case made of glazed porcelain.

Chronometer: An accurate timekeeper.

Clock: A machine that records the passing of time and strikes at least on the hour.

Clockwise: The direction in which the clock hands rotate around the dial.

Connecticut Shelf Clock: Any shelf clock made in Connecticut, such as a beehive, cottage, or steeple clock.

Cornice: The horizontal molded projection at the top of a clock case.

Count Wheel: The locking plate that controls the number of strikes on a clock's bell or gong.

Crystal Regulator Clock: A shelf clock with glass panels on all four sides.

Date Dial: An additional dial that shows the dates of the month.

Deadbeat Escapement: A clock escapement that does not recoil (fall back).

Dial: A clock's face, with numbers and hands.

Drum: In a weight-driven clock, the round barrel on which the weight cord is wound.

Ebonized: Having a black finish that looks like ebony wood.

Eight-Day Clock: A clock that runs for eight days on one winding.

Escapement: The clock mechanism that controls the swing of the pendulum or the movement of the balance wheel.

Escutcheon: The trim around a keyhole.

Finial: A wooden or metal spire or turning.

Flying Pendulum Clock: Also referred to as an Ignatz clock, a novelty clock invented in 1883 and reproduced in the late 1950s. Hanging from an arm, a small ball on a thread acts as a pendulum by swinging in a horizontal circle and twisting and untwisting around vertical rods on each side of the clock.

Four-Hundred-Day Clock: A clock that runs a full year on a single winding. It is also called an anniversary clock.

Frame: The case of a clock.

Front Wind: A clock that is wound through an opening in the dial.

Fusee or Fuzee: A grooved cone on which the cord from the spring container unwinds to equalize the force of the spring in a clock.

Gadget Clock: A clock with accessories.

Gallery Clock: An eight-day or electric clock, usually round, with a simple case and a dial usually eight inches or larger designed to hang on a wall in a public place.

Gilt: A gold-colored coating.

Gimbal: A support used to keep a clock level.

Gingerbread: The name used to describe the elaborate designs pressed into a clock's wooden case.

Gold Leaf: An extremely thin sheet of solid gold sometimes applied as a decoration on columns, tablets, or other parts of a clock case.

Gothic Case: A case shaped like a Gothic arch; also called a beehive clock because its sloping sides give it an apprearance similar to a beehive.

Grandfather Clock: The name for a floor standing clock in a tall, upright case; originally called a long-case or tall-case clock.

Grandmother Clock: A smaller, floor-standing version of a grandfather clock.

Hairspring: A slender hair-like coil that controls the regular movement of the balance wheel in a clock.

Hammer: The clock part that hits the bell or gong to indicate time.

Hands: The time indicators that mark the hours, minutes, and seconds on a clock dial.

Hanging Shelf Clock: A wall clock with a shelf-like base that makes it appear as if it is resting on a shelf.

Horology: The science of measuring time or making timepieces.

Hourglass: A device containing sand that flows from the upper to the lower globe to indicate the passing of a certain amount of time.

Ignatz Clock: See Flying Pendulum Clock.

Iron-Front Clock: A shelf clock with a front made of cast-iron.

Kidney Dial: A dial on a clock that resembles the shape of a kidney.

Kitchen Clock: A clock frequently of oak, manufactured from the late 1800s to the early 1900s, that was commonly placed on a shelf in a kitchen.

Jack: A moving figure turned by a clock mechanism.

Leaves: The teeth of pinion gears.

Lighthouse Clock: A unique clock made by Simon Willard in 1822, featuring an octagonal base, a mahogany case, a tapered circular trunk, and a glass dome covering an eight-day alarm movement.

Long-Case Clock: The original name for a grand-father clock.

Looking-Glass Clock: A clock with a box-like case and mirror instead of a painted-glass tablet.

Lyre Clock: A form of banjo clock with a lyre shape.

Mainspring: A coiled wire that provides the prin-cipal tension or driving power to keep the movement running in a spring-driven clock.

Mantel Clock: A shelf clock.

Marine or Lever Clock: A clock that operates with a hairspring balance and continues to run when transported or set on an uneven surface (unlike pendulum clocks); often used aboard ships.

Marquetry: A form of decoration made by inlaying wood veneers in various designs.

Mask: A human or animal face used as a decoration.

Massachusetts Shelf Clock: A style of clock frequently called half-clock or box-on-box.

Mean Time: When all hours and days are of equal time.

Medallion: An applied circular, oval, or square decorative turning used on a clock case.

Mercury Pendulum: In American clocks, a silvery-looking, usually cylindrical pendulum designed to simulate French examples, which actually contained mercury.

Mirror Clock: Also known as a looking-glass clock.

Mission-Style Clock: A clock with a plain, straight-lined case made of oak, popular from about 1900 to 1925.

Molding: A continuous decorative edging.

Moon Dial: The dial at the top of a clock that shows the phases of the moon.

Movement: The "works" of a clock.

Musical Alarm: An alarm that plays a tune on a small musical box. It was popular from the late 1890s to about 1915.

Novelty Clock: A small, often animated clock, usually in the shape of a familiar object.

OG (Ogee) Clock: A double, continuous S-like curve used as a molding on certain straight rectangular clocks of the early 1800s.

Open Escapement: The wheel and pallet movement that can be seen on some clock dials.

Pallet: A catching device that regulates the speed of a clock by releasing one notch of a toothed wheel (ratchet wheel) at each swing of the pendulum or turn of the balance wheel.

Parlor Clock: The carved-case Victorian clock of the mid-to-late 1800s, typically made of walnut, designed to be placed on a shelf or mantel in the parlor.

Pediment: An ornamental top on a clock case, frequently curved in shape.

Pendulum: A clock weight hung from a fixed point, which swings back and forth in a regular beat to regulate a clock's movement.

Pillar-and-Scroll Clock: A shelf clock attributed to Eli Terry, having a column on each side, a scroll-cut pediment and three finials on top.

Pinion: A small toothed wheel driven by a gear.

Plate: The front and back of the clock's movement or works.

Position Clock: Also called a regulator clock.

Regulator Clock: Originally a term for any highly accurate clock.

Reverse Painting: A picture or design often used on a clock tablet and painted on the back side of a glass in reverse order of a normal painting.

Roman Numerals: Roman letters used as numerals on clock dials, such as I, II, III, IV, etc. On older clocks, four was often represented by IIII, an old Roman numeral for IV. It is said that this form better balances the VIII on the other side of the dial.

Shelf Clock: A clock designed to sit on a shelf or mantel.

Spandrels: The four corners that square off a round clock dial, often featuring painted designs or metal decorations.

Spring-Driven Clock: A clock whose power is provided by springs, rather than falling weights.

Steeple Clock: A clock with a sharply pointed Gothic case, and two or four finials at each side forming spires.

Sweep Second Hand: A hand positioned in the center of the clock that sweeps, in a circular motion, around the dial; also called center seconds hand.

Tablet: The front, lower glass, frequently painted, on a clock case.

Tall Clock: A long-case floor clock, often called a grandfather clock.

Tambour Clock: A shelf clock, also called a

humback or camelback clock, with a case that is rounded in the middle and gently slopes to flat sides.

Thirty-Day Clock: A clock that runs for a month on a single winding.

Time and Strike (T & S) Clock: A clock that both tells the time and strikes or chimes.

Timepiece: A clock that tells time only and does not strike or chime.

TP: An abbreviation for timepiece.

Tower or Turret Clock: A church, steeple, or public clock in a tower.

Train: The series of gears and pinions that transfer power to the escapement.

Verge: The pallet axis of a clock.

Visible Escapement: Same as open escapement.

Wagon Spring: A series of flat springs, attributed to Joseph Ives of Bristol, Connecticut, used instead of a coil spring to power a clock movement.

Wall Clock: A clock designed to hang on a wall.

Weight-Driven Clock: A clock that uses heavy objects suspended from the works by chain or spring to power the clock movement as they drop. A spring-driven clock, on the other hand, relies on the tension of a coiled wire to provide power.

Winker: An iron statue clock with blinking eyes.

Zebrawood: A striped, straw-colored African wood that is sliced into veneers to cover an unattractive wood; also called zebrano.

Bibliography

BOOKS

Bailey, Chris H. *Two Hundred Years of American Clocks and Watches*. Englewood Cliffs, N.J.: A Rutledge Book, Prentice-Hall, no date.

Brewer, Clifford. *Pocket Book of Clocks*. Felthan, Middlesex, England: Country Life Books, an imprint of Newes Books, a division of the Hamlyn Publishing Group Ltd., 1983.

Burton, Eric. *Clocks and Watches 1400-1900*. New York and Washington: Frederick A. Praeger Publishers, no date.

Distin, William H., and Robert Bishop. *The American Clock*. New York: E. P. Dutton, 1976.

Drepperd, Carl W. *American Clocks and Clock Makers*. Garden City, N.Y.: Doubleday & Company, 1947.

Ehrhardt, Roy. *Official Price Guide to Antique Clocks*. Westminster: The House of Collectibles, 1985.

Ehrhardt, Roy, and Red Rabeneck. *Clock Identification and Price Guide*. Kansas City, Mo.: Heart of America Press, 1983.

Lloyd, Alan H. *The Collector's Dictionary of Clocks*. New York: A. S. Barnes and Co., 1964.

Ly, Tran Duy. *Clocks: A Guide to Identification and Prices*. Arlington, Va.: 1984.

Maust, Don, ed. *Early American Clocks*. Union Town, Pa.: E. G. Warman Publishing Co., 1971.

Mebane, John. *The Coming Collecting Boon*. New York: A. S. Barnes and Company, 1968.

Miller, Andrew Hayes, and Dalia Marcia Miller. *Survey of American Clocks: Calendar Clocks*. Elgin, Ill. Antiquitat, 1972.

Miller, Robert W. *Clock Guide Identification with Prices*. Des Moines, Iowa: Wallace-Homestead Book Company, 1974.

------------ *Clock Guide No. 2, Identification with Prices*. Des Moines, Iowa: Wallace-Homestead Book Company, 1975.

Moore, Hudson N. *The Old Clock Book*. New York: Tudor Publishing Company, 1936.

Palmer, Brooks. *The Book of American Clocks*. New York: The Macmillan Company, 1974.

------------ *A Treasury of American Clocks*. New York: The Macmillan Company, 1968.

Schwartz, Marvin D. *Collectors' Guide to Antique American Clocks*. Garden City, N.Y.: Doubleday & Company, Inc., 1975.

Smith, Alan, ed. *The International Dictionary of Clocks*. London, Auckland, Melbourne, Singapore, and Toronto: 1988.

Welch, Kenneth F. *The History of Clocks and Watches*. New York: Drake Publishers, Inc., 1972.

CATALOGS

Israel, Fred L., ed. *1897 Sears, Roebuck Catalogue*. New York: Chelsea House Publishers, 1976.

F. Kroeber Clock Co. Manufacturers Catalogue of Clocks, New York, 1898.

Ly, Tran Duy. *Chelsea Clock Co. Catalog E 1911*. Arlington, Va.: Arlington Horology & Book Co., 1987.

Schroeder, Joseph J., Jr., ed. *1908 Sears, Roebuck Catalogue*. Chicago, Ill.: The Gun Digest Company, 1969.

NEWSLETTERS

"Eli Terry: Dreamer, Artisan and Clockmaker," Bulletin of the National Association of Watch and Clock Collectors, Inc., summer 1965.

"The Welch, Spring and Company," Bulletin of the National Association of Watch and Clock Collectors, Inc., #12, February 1978.

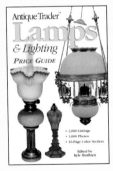
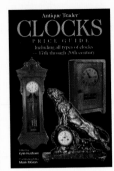
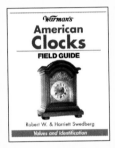
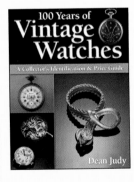